To my daughter and my son never give up on your dreams
and always be brave.

Jolene Roberts

HOW BIG IS YOUR BRAVE?

AUSTIN MACAULEY PUBLISHERS™

LONDON • CAMBRIDGE • NEW YORK • SHARJAH

Ordering Information
Quantity sales: Special discounts are available on quantity purchases by corporations, associations, and others. For details, contact the publisher at the address below.

Publisher's Cataloging-in-Publication data
Roberts, Jolene
How Big is Your Brave?

ISBN 9798889103103 (Paperback)
ISBN 9798889103110 (Hardback)
ISBN 9798889103127 (ePub e-book)

Library of Congress Control Number: 2023916931

www.austinmacauley.com/us

First Published 2024
Austin Macauley Publishers LLC
40 Wall Street, 33rd Floor, Suite 3302
New York, NY 10005
USA

mail-usa@austinmacauley.com
+1 (646) 5125767

Author's Note

The names and characteristics of the people in this book have been altered to protect them, but also to take liberty with their stories in order to help the reader understand their motivations. These stories are told from my perspective only, which allows me to make assumptions based upon the many years I have spent in the fitness industry.

In the process, I've witnessed a lot of crazy perceptions, followed by a lot of crazy actions.

I hope this book will help you avoid some of those behaviors and, instead, help you find your way.

Introduction

How Big is Your Brave? came from a desire I had to show that completing two Ironman competitive races by a middle-aged, out-of-shape, divorced mother of two, was no different than many of the daunting tasks my friends, peers, co-workers and strangers have also overcome in their daily lives.

I began this quest by asking friends, family, clients and sometimes strangers what was their "Ironman"? What were they putting off doing in their lives that was a call coming from their soul? What fears were stopping them in their tracks?

I found that many were struggling to recognize their fears, or find their purpose despite the fact that when we take on fear, face our Ironman, and dig in, our purpose can begin to emerge. Yet, I knew all too well that task was easier said than done. My own fears had been tucked away far too long. Bringing them forward would, I thought, require more strength than I possessed.

I was wrong. This book will show you how I found the strength I thought I didn't have.

First, I had to learn what fear is and isn't.

Faith, bravery, and courage are not the absence of fear. They are the fabric of what we use to move when our body says stand still. Faith allows your heart to believe in spite of what you think you know.

Faith is one of my favorite strengths. I use it to move into places I never thought I could be. Faith requires the power of perception to see the victory through the fire and smoke. The power of perceptions is what allows the light to shine out, the light that others see in us that helps them to rally behind us, or cheer for us in spite of what they may feel about our choices.

I have always known I wanted to spend my life helping people, though I wasn't sure what that would look like. After graduating college in 1992 with a degree in law enforcement, I tried my hand as a juvenile probation and parole officer. But I quickly learned that wasn't what I wanted to do for the rest of my life.

So, I began searching for a new "next". In 1993, I interviewed for a position teaching English as a second language in Seoul, South Korea. This job was a better fit for me, and I left the U.S. a few months later to begin my role as a traveling teacher. Along the way, I hoped to find myself and wake the sleeping giant I always felt lay deep within me.

Overseas is where I met my husband, who was in the military in Korea. Within a year, we were married and leaving for Germany. For the next five years, I taught English as a second language in community college, for the Air Force, and through private lessons before returning home to the U.S.

In 1999, my daughter was born and I began a full-time commitment to motherhood. I also realized I had a lifelong passion for fitness and teaching aerobics classes. Prior to having my daughter, I had dabbled in teaching step, floor and water aerobics teaching classes a few times a week. But like many women, having a child changed everything for me.

Not only did I have a chance to teach aerobics classes, giving me an important outlet as a full-time mother, I could be my newest, best client. Pregnancy, in fact, had done me no favors in terms of my body. It was not a good time for me physically. While many women glow and bask in this stage of motherhood, I was ballooning up and feeling miserable.

Only a month after my daughter's birth, I was called in to teach fitness classes. Despite the shame of my two hundred pounds, and knowing my normal weight (about a hundred forty pounds) was at least six months away, I gathered up my courage and agreed to teach again.

I needed to get out and stop hiding. I also wanted to motivate myself through motivating others. Over time, I learned everything I could about fitness, earning nearly a dozen different certifications and completing a number of health-related workshops.

Staying active isn't a stretch for me as I've been active most of my life. I played volleyball in high school, tennis with my parents, and soccer on a co-ed team. I have always enjoyed being outside and working out. It makes me feel good, so loving physical activity is easy.

However, our family was divided when it came to wellness and fitness. My dad and I were active, my mom and sister not so much. My mom taught swimming lessons, but didn't seem to enjoy physical activity as much as my father and I did. She was a reader who crocheted and loved nothing more than sitting quietly or puttering around the house.

She was the best mother and was always home when we got home. She made sure we had snacks and a hot meal for dinner each night. She was an amazing cook and baker and I know that didn't help her with her weight.

I also watched as my father, who went from being slightly and silently annoyed at my mother for her steady weight gain. I believe my dad thought he could motivate her with his criticism, but not surprisingly, what resulted was a situation in which my mom ate to avoid the stress of her unhappiness. The more he complained, the more she ate, stuffing her emotions in the unhealthiest way possible.

This delicate dance between my parents was a cross between loving each other and resenting each other over her weight issues. It was then I formed an opinion that in marriage, love was not always unconditional. I also began to believe that being overweight in a marriage would only make marriage more difficult.

I love both my parents and I think they did the best they could in difficult circumstances. Still married after fifty years, they disagree about the same issues, but somehow, and thankfully, it works for them. My mom has lost some weight over the years, though I still try to nudge her in the right direction.

My dad is not as hard-core as he once was, but he still goes to the gym several times a week. I concluded they must have been doing something right, and that I should love them both just the way they are.

Besides, shaming never works.

Due to my parental influence, I decided I would not marry someone who cared so much about my weight. Yet, I stepped right into the same type of relationship, as though it was a comfortable shoe, and wore it for more than twenty years.

Weight became an issue that put a crack in the foundation of our marriage. It was one of the many issues that ultimately ended our marriage.

When something big happens, it shakes you to the very core—like an earthquake with a fault line that runs down the center of who you are. I felt I was forced to clean up after the destruction because leaving it in pieces seemed more painful.

I have since learned that the root cause of my fear comes from believing I am not enough.

I always needed to do more, achieve more, and work harder to be what I thought others saw. When fear is your focus, emotion transforms into energy in motion, creating an endless loop of fear, emotion, and energy that can entrap you for decades.

Over the years, I also learned that, at least for me, fear is a two-sided coin involving the power and the poison of perception. The motivation for most everything I do seems to vacillate between the two—how do I avoid the poison of the perception of others while using its positive power to my advantage?

Coming to terms with my fear has given me courage. After the divorce, which clearly changed my life dramatically, I finally became a willing participant in my life. I was no longer shielded by others' perceptions nor pummeled by my own faulty perceptions. Instead, I was forced to sit down with the storyteller I had carried around in my head for years.

I was given the opportunity and the ability to create my new life and my new normal. The challenge would be, would I take it? What would it look like to live a life with less fear? Am I worthy of the time it will take to dismantle the very fears I felt had moved me to greatness?

Completing two Ironman races, starting over successfully with personal training, teaching yoga and selling real estate. Would they crush me or make me stronger?

Fear revealed has become, for me, like the moment in *The Wizard of Oz* when Toto pulls back the curtain to reveal the wizard. I felt pure relief while watching the scene when we discover he's not a fire-breathing wizard. He's just a man.

One of my favorite quotes comes from the final scenes when the Tin Man asks the Wizard for a heart and the Wizard replies, "A heart will never be practical until it can be made unbreakable." Facing and conquering fear requires risk and the risk can be a heart that can be shattered. But we move forward anyway. That's courage.

Slowly but surely, it became clearer that I was the only one who thought that I wasn't enough.

Unlike the Tin Man, I found I didn't need an unbreakable heart. I needed courage like the Lion. I have a strong heart and I love hard and I am passionate. I began reading books, taking online classes and learning new ways to cope and be a better version of myself. As I have become better acquainted with myself, I have learned that I hide my heart behind a big curtain and hope it never gets hurt.

I have accomplished many things, but never with the risks of a broken heart. In all my years of doing great things, I may have been avoiding standing still to let life pass through me. I haven't really allowed things that could harm me to come near me, including my relationships.

My fitness level and my superstar moments may have been a way to avoid being ordinary. As I dig deeper, my chasing after and accomplishing big dreams may have simply been the numbing that is the same for drug addicts or alcoholics. I needed to find a way to ask for help, but I had created a personality and life that reflected no help was needed. Just recently in a very innocuous way, my inability to ask for help took me on a path I didn't expect.

After the dust had settled and my Ironman days were behind me, I began to realize that I was not as motivated and as driven as I had been. I began to beat myself up and do things to punish myself for not being the best version of myself I could be. I call these moments being lost; wandering in the desert.

I felt disoriented. The path was no longer visible. I felt heavy and uncomfortable. My steps were labored and I couldn't figure out how I got here. The map I had used in the past didn't have the current places I was visiting. I had no idea how to get out.

This kind of lost was different from the wilderness kind of lost. I was lost in the same spot I was standing in. The things I was afraid of were all inside of me, and the journey was into new terrain.

To be more specific, I felt fat and uncomfortable. I was not even sure how I got here, but I knew at that moment it mattered less how I got here and became more a question of—how do I get to where I want to be?

I began reading *Deep Survival*, by Laurence Gonzales. It's a *riveting* book about people who have been lost at sea, lost in the woods, trapped on mountains, and in plane crashes. Its lessons gave me a new perspective. I was captivated by the book and how it paralleled my situation.

The author goes on to explain that there are three things people do when they are in trouble. The first thing is panic, then they forget the plan, and finally they are paralyzed and stop moving altogether, which often leads to their death.

As I read each page, I could feel this book outlining how I felt. The difference was, I was lost in my own skin. I had skills I wasn't using. I was also starting to hope I would be rescued before I stopped moving and froze.

This part of my life made it possible for me to release the need for a pre-made map, a compass made by the perception of others. As a result, I've now given myself permission to wander as needed. I'm not confused about what got me here—my striving, my unworthy feelings, my ambitious need to prove something to everyone.

Those things were wrapped as tight as Spandex by one single, powerful word: fear. I learned that much of my drive was born from the opinion of others.

As I slowed down enough to catch a glimpse of myself in the mirror, I could see that I was exhausted and essentially going nowhere. My fat had become my fortress and my new hiding place. I realized that my attempts to make the inside and the outside match would require less reflecting out and more reflecting in.

I didn't think I could ask for help because I am a trainer. I have been fit for over twenty years and I can do strong and powerful things. But during this period, I wasn't as focused at the gym. I was struggling to manage my weight and in the midst of my panic trying to maintain a calm demeanor.

I told friends that I was letting my body heal after two Ironman races. I made excuses for my weight gain, saying my age made it possible that I could be experiencing menopause. I was afraid that something was wrong but didn't really want to ask for help. The poison of my false perception began to wear away at my resolve.

Finally, I went to have routine hormone tests done. I was elated to find out I had almost run out of testosterone (Not really, but I like that picture versus low testosterone). My doctor recommended a treatment plan and within five days, I felt like my old self again.

I couldn't believe the time I had wasted beating myself up and how easy the fix was for my issue. All that time, my fear kept me from enjoying my own freedom.

I realize that not every story is that simple to fix, which is why I wanted to write this book. Fear is fear and fixing it comes from facing it. I needed help and I asked for it. It took great effort to sit in a room and tell someone that I felt helpless. I thought about the times clients came to me and told me how sick and tired they were of being sick and tired.

I knew the courage it took for them to ask for help and I made sure they knew I would help. I, however, would do everything I could do to *avoid* asking for help. I know where

I have been in my heart, when I was afraid to say I needed help. Now, asking for help has become a victory.

Through that experience, I have come to believe fear can be an opportunity to learn about faith and what we believe in, including ourselves. I was fortunate to have personal victories, but I sometimes wonder if they kept me from this moment when I would stop running from myself?

While fear is worthwhile in some situations, it's mostly a way to keep ourselves from really living. Fear builds walls to keep others out. We stay trapped by the fear we create. We make the fear real, and give it a story we can run with until we have to face it.

Only then do we realize it wasn't real at all. Giving yourself permission to experience and dissect your fears can lead you to an inner purpose that more closely matches your outer purpose.

I am hoping the stories in this book will move you to look at what fear does to you and why. You will be forced to ask yourself what you have been sacrificing to keep fear close and other, important people and things at bay.

Ask yourself what keeps you from being your best self. What if you fail? More importantly: What if you succeed? What if, in facing your fears, you find there was nothing there?

I know all too well that fear is what we create so we don't have to dig in and do the hard work. Diet and exercise seem like hard work and many people resist it, saying they don't like the regimen of diet or exercise. But in the years that I have worked with my clients, I've discovered the hard work isn't about food or activity.

It's about taking risks, facing your fears, and knowing that all the work you do could change everything, or it could change nothing. But you are still victorious in the end because you made the effort.

It's about recognizing that perception of yourself—which you have control over, and the perception from others—which you have no control over, can be either a poisonous path or a path to real freedom. It's your choice.

My fears haven't gone away. I still wrestle with them daily, but now I invite them in like long-lost friends, friends not there to harm me, but to teach me.

Maya Angelou once wrote that when you know better, you do better. I am learning to know better and am always trying to do better, despite new fears that continuously show themselves.

Fear will challenge you, change you, or crush you. It can be your best friend or your worst enemy, and sometimes it can be both. The people who shared their stories and their fears with me also changed their lives.

To that end, I hope you will see a little of yourself in every story and every client.

Chapter One
Momma Bear

I always wanted to raise my children in an environment where *healthy* is the theme and making good choices is the method. But parenting, though the most rewarding job in the world, is also the toughest. There are so many responsibilities, from how to instill important values to how to properly feed a child. I've found that loving and caring for children is a job for the brave.

Early on, I introduced healthy food in our home, including vegetables, fruits, and the merits of moderation. In my own childhood, I was taught to eat what was prepared or go without, so I followed that model with my children, and by and large, it worked.

Since my mom is a fantastic cook, it wasn't difficult to eat what was placed in front of me. We had pinto beans and cornbread most Monday nights and always had some type of goulash (my mom's version of leftovers reincarnated into a new dinner).

This was in the late seventies and early eighties when the convenience and availability of fast food, along with latchkey kids (children whose parents worked and let themselves in the house), weren't as prominent. Today, obesity in children has risen to epic proportions due to many factors. As a result, children are not only dealing with their unhealthy weight, but the social stigma that goes along with it.

It begs the question: Who is responsible for the obese child? The parent who buys the food and decides what the child is offered, or the child who makes the choice to eat the food and consumes too much of it?

That question was brought home to me in a real-life example when I met Nick at the high school that hosted my son's preschool program.

First, a little background.

When my daughter was in kindergarten, I came to her class as a volunteer, providing a fitness break for the kids. As part of my routine, I set up an obstacle course, instructed the kids in physical activities, and shared information about how they could make healthier food choices.

To be honest, I was pretty convinced it would not be a hundred percent successful. After all, it required a shift in responsibility, some blame, and a lot of marketing genius to fix the problems inherent in our food and fitness industry.

Much like the current opioid crisis, it's hard to identify who is at fault or where the solutions lie. Never mind that our young people are dying from a drug epidemic at faster rates than ever before. With childhood obesity, as with drugs, we are afraid that identifying parents as the "culprit" will cause far greater issues than finding a solution.

For example, in 2014, my county conducted a government-led study in which body mass index (BMI) was tested in elementary schools for more than 13,000 children over a prescribed period of time. Recognizing that normal weight for a typical six-year-old is about fifty pounds, a number of these children were identified as obese if they weighed ninety pounds or more.

But even after categorizing these children as statistically unhealthy due to their obesity, they were not provided follow-up and guidance. Why? Because parents were not informed. No one in the study wanted to be the "bad guy" by revealing to parents their child was at a dangerously unhealthy weight.

Year after year, our county collected the data and submitted the information. Yet only wellness experts were privy to the results, and the data contained within the study was used only to provide statistical information to state agencies. This seemed crazy to me.

What is the right answer? Who are the right people to take on this complex problem? Though I am uncertain of the "right" answers, I knew I had the ability then and now to make a difference.

That's where Nick enters the story. My son attended preschool at the local high school. The students would learn aspects of child care earning high school credit and my son enjoyed preschool with the students. As I drove my son back and forth to preschool that year, I noticed a young man sitting on a bench in the afternoon sun.

He was obese by any standards (I would later learn at five feet four, he weighed 434 pounds), taking in deep breaths before lumbering across the street to catch his bus.

Over time, I began to look for him regularly and when I did, I wondered: Isn't anyone helping him? If so, why wouldn't they say something to him? Where was the P.E.

teacher, the school nurse, or the school counselor? What about his family?

Month after month he sat on that same bench, appearing to get larger. And no one seemed to be doing anything about it. What, I thought, must it feel like for this young man to breathe with all that weight bearing down on his chest?

I see this same dynamic when a member of a family needs to take a hard look at their weight and make changes. Loved ones feel they can't say anything. The fear of telling someone they are wrong to be fat or they aren't taking care of themselves seems to be greater than the consequences of watching someone die from the inside out.

As a fitness trainer, I found it incredibly difficult to watch Nick physically labor to cross the street. The energy it took to move his body alone was more than most fit people expend during an exercise routine. Carrying all that weight had to be hard on his bones. Often, he would rock from side to side as if needing momentum just to get up from the bench.

How long could he continue to live that way? Had he already developed diabetes or hypertension? I thought, *this boy's body is killing him.* Yet, I still held back from saying anything as the weeks wore on.

Why do we hold back the care and concern to preserve someone's feelings? The fear of telling someone what we see from the outside can hold others hostage to the loved one battling obesity. It's a tricky dance.

Many people I speak with say they need to be in good physical shape before they can judge another person through speaking out. But let's turn that around. What if the pressure they put on someone else results in their own needed changes? Wouldn't that be a win-win for everyone?

Truth and honesty are two different things. Truth can cut like a knife, have no real boundaries, and be based on assumptions. Honesty comes from the heart and is often coupled with the best of intentions. If we were all honest (and kind) to one another, could we also be more helpful? Sometimes you have to take risks where honesty is involved—taking the risk of offending someone in order to help them.

Our children need us to be good examples and help them make wise choices. It's often too late to help by the time kids are obese. They have already formed their personalities, beliefs, and eating habits by around the age of six.

According to a 2018 report from the Trust for America's Health, thirteen percent of all children are severely obese by the ages of six to eleven, with obesity being linked to a number of health problems, including diabetes, high blood pressure, stroke, and heart disease.

In Nick's case, what must it be like to feel as though you are only surviving at such a young age? I wondered if he felt trapped, drowning in depths as heavy as his weight. As a mother, my heart ached for him. If he were my son, how would I fix this?

It was then I began to feel more afraid of what would happen if I *didn't* help him. Yet I still wasn't yet ready to say anything. I had my own fears to work through before I could reach out to another person. Would he and his family be receptive? Would they actually want my help?

And who was I to think I could help?

I knew from my own high school experience that the drama and gossip among "normal" kids was epic. Was he the topic of regular teasing and cruel antics? What would kids say and do to this young man to make his situation worse?

Many of us have been the butt of someone's joke and everyone laughs at our expense. I wondered if he was picked on daily. I wondered what his peers said to him and if they were afraid to be his friend because of his size.

The end of the school year was approaching as I continued to wait for the "right time" to talk with Nick. Thinking someone else would take care of his problem was part of my denial and inertia. In retrospect, I knew my stalling meant I wouldn't have to step up and do it myself. I also knew I had the ability and the desire to help. I just needed to overcome my fear of reaching out.

One day, I realized it was now or never; time to make a commitment rather than sit there and idly watch this young man struggle. Yet even as a trainer, it was not easy for me to walk up to a stranger and say, 'Hey, you need me.' Neither is it a particularly good way to gain new friends or clients.

I wrestled with what to say that would make an impact on this vulnerable boy. Would he be offended? Would he scream at me? Would he be upset or angry? Weighing all these emotions caused me to experience a fear that almost made me change my mind.

I finally decided that I would not allow the fear of offending him paralyze me, using the fear of what would happen instead if I didn't help this precious young man. That particular fear was a better motivator. But it wasn't easy. Though I was learning fear can help move you in the direction you need to go, I continued to waffle before actually making a move.

Still uncertain, I left the situation up to fate. If I saw him on my next trip to the school, I would say something. If I didn't, I was off the hook. I knew I would have only a split second to make a decision on what I would say before I approached him.

That day, I drove toward the school with trepidation. Anxiously, I looked toward the bench. There he was, same as always. With nothing rehearsed, I grabbed a business card, got out of the car, and went toward him.

He looked up as I approached. His large brown eyes on full alert.

'I don't know if anyone has ever told you this,' I began, 'but if you don't lose weight, you are probably going to die. Please have your mother call me.' I handed him the card, turned around, and left as quickly as I came.

Yep, similar to the stuff that falls out of your bag when you turn a sharp corner, the words fell right out of my mouth and I had no idea how they would land, or what the consequences would be. If his mother called me, it was meant to be. If she didn't, again I was off the hook.

However, it wasn't long before my phone rang. Nick's mother's first words after introducing herself were, 'Okay, what's the catch?' I could sense her cynicism through the phone, as sharp and thick as a hunting blade. I understood her implied perception: *Why would a strange lady offer to help her son and what does this woman want in return?*

I wondered if she felt I had judged her as a mother or made unfair assumptions. All the thoughts and fears I had about reaching out came rushing back to me during that phone call. I so wanted to help; my heart was genuine. But in a world full of B.S. and empty promises, I knew this was no small hill to climb.

And I can't say I blamed her. I might have reacted exactly the same. In fact, I believe I was as afraid of meeting her as she was of me.

I also wondered why she should trust me. I knew only time would tell. First impressions are always critical and often set the stage for how we treat people. As the days passed, we spoke again, her hard shell slowly beginning to crack. Finally, she agreed that I could meet her family in person.

Nick's mother was about her son's height (five feet three) yet weighed more than two hundred pounds. His sister was five feet tall and she, too, tipped the scales at twice her normal weight. Nick's stepfather came to the meeting as well. He was a small man, short and slender, weighing less than I did.

I thought how strange that such a physically small man was part of such a big family. He didn't participate much in the conversation, and I was soon aware that he would probably not take part in the fitness plan we were discussing for his family.

Yet I knew this wasn't about the stepfather. It was about Nick and his well-being.

As I began working with Nick, my impressions of him began to change. He had a beautiful face with bright eyes that lit up whenever he smiled or appeared surprised. I could also tell that from his hesitancy to smile and interact, he had adopted others' skewed perceptions of him. He referred to himself as "fat", "worthless", and other self-defeating, inaccurate descriptions.

'Because I'm fat, there's nothing about me that's beautiful,' he'd often say.

I tried to counter his negativity, telling him his face was the frame that allowed his soul to shine through when he smiled. But with each compliment, he shook his head, allowing the opinion of others to convince him he wasn't good enough. In that sense, he was victimized twice, first by the poisonous perception of others, and then by his inability to recognize and value his own worth.

Mostly fueled by fear, our feelings about ourselves keep us from coming out of the corner of the room—like a child who's hiding from their parents for fear of punishment.

Making matters worse for Nick, he had a terrible stutter, so at our first meeting, the conversation was labored and difficult for him. I can only imagine that this complicated his ability to fit in at school and elsewhere. There was irony at work here—people who want to blend in don't feel like they have a voice.

Was Nick's stutter just another way for him to disappear into the background or for him to be the target of others' cruelty?

My plan as a trainer was to work with Nick first, then help his family members by assigning homework and having them work together as a team. No whining and no complaining were allowed. And I told Nick, 'When you quit, I quit. That means the end result is up to you.'

Throughout that summer, we worked together on a weekly basis, walking on the treadmill, lifting weights, taking hikes and swimming in the pool at his complex.

When I learned Nick was using his daytime hours to primarily sit and watch TV instead of following through on his assignments, I invited him to my house, where I could devote my time exclusively to him.

Almost every week, there were new obstacles to overcome, some of which I never anticipated. For instance, my equipment was not commercial grade, and not suited for his enormous weight. I struggled with how to explain the problem without making him feel worse than he did already. In the end, I decided to say nothing and pray the manufacturers had underestimated the maximum weight allowance.

He eventually learned to pace himself walking on the treadmill and working the elliptical machine. We also took nature walks when the weather allowed—a new experience for him as he was fearful of being outside.

'My family doesn't go outside much,' he explained.

Then there was the issue of food. Nick was having difficulty changing his eating habits, and at first, I couldn't understand why. We had discussed healthy eating at great length, and Nick's mother agreed his diet would require drastic change. Yet week after week, the pounds refused to come off.

There had to be something else going on. I soon learned what it was.

I repeatedly asked Nick if he was following a recommended diet at family dinners.

'Well,' he hedged. 'We go to grandma's every Sunday and I eat stuff that isn't good for me.'

He finally explained that his family would think him rude if he didn't eat the same things they did. Those things included fried food, mashed potatoes, heaping bowls of gravy, biscuits, and a large variety of desserts. He ate along with them because, he said, he didn't want to make the people he loved feel bad. As a result, he was sacrificing his own goals so that others would be "okay".

The same thing had happened at school, he added. The lunch ladies felt bad for him, sensing he was lonely and isolated. While they couldn't give him friends, they could certainly give him extra helpings of food, none of which he felt he could refuse.

That was an eye-opening experience for me, a glimpse into the role psychology and family dynamics play in our quest for healthy eating habits and culture.

I began to ask Nick, along with other clients who faced similar challenges, how getting healthier might affect his family for the good. 'What if,' I asked, 'you didn't help them feel better by giving in, but by allowing them to witness the changes in you?'

Though Nick agreed, it was still a vicious cycle and an ongoing battle, one I believed I was unlikely to win. We never discussed this, but I also knew there were cultural differences at play. In some ethnic families, there is no stigma if you happen to be large. They love big, live big, and eat big, all of which is perfectly fine if you can overlook the health consequences that often follow excessive eating.

How could I help Nick get unstuck with so many uphill battles? I worked with him and his family for more than two years. We did everything from shopping in the grocery store, completing local 5k races to sharing holidays, summers, and special events. Nick even attended overnight camp two summers in a row, something he never thought he would be able to do.

During our time together, I learned many things about him, and many things from him, creating a bond of affection and respect along the way. I learned from him that we each have a battle, a journey and oftentimes a destiny, and no one can do it for us. We must do it for ourselves and by ourselves. I learned that Nick had a generous heart and a kind soul wedged in that massive frame.

I learned he was afraid people would let him down and often they did. I took from my experience with Nick, the deep need to really connect with one another as we help them on their journey, they in turn help us. While Nick lost a tremendous amount of weight (losing over 150 pounds), he also got healthier and stronger.

Perhaps more importantly, he learned to overcome his poor perception of himself and the fear of failure that had kept him imprisoned from childhood on.

When I last caught up with Nick, he was engaged in drawing fashion designs and dreaming about his future. His newfound strength allowed him to fight for the life he wanted to grow into. He wasn't there yet, by any stretch, but he now had goals, and a new vision of himself with new possibilities.

There is a power in learning about yourself and changing the way you live in order to reach a healthier outlook. It's a shift that requires more effort than most realize.

Nick is still maintaining healthier habits, eating healthy foods and exercising, in his daily life, but has regained some of the weight he lost. We have since talked about the inner strength he will need to manage his weight throughout the course of his life. Losing weight and gaining inner strength will always be an uncertain path for him.

But he seemed happier and more upbeat than I had seen him in the past.

For all of us, the journey to becoming our best selves is not an easy one and is often marred by the sins of the past. Fortunately, Nick is a young man with his whole life ahead of him and knows that the choices he makes today will help shape and direct all of his tomorrows.

Overall, I am satisfied with the work Nick and I completed together. I have only a few regrets, but those are things beyond my control. I wish I had helped him sooner. I wish I had been able to teach his family how to help him be more successful.

I would have preferred that he had greater weight loss over time, and maintained the loss. I wish that my lessons on nutrition had taken root and planted new eating habits in his early, formative years.

However, I now know that my inner drive to constantly do "better" is more about me than about him, and is a part of my journey, too. I have to remind myself that I overcame my fear of approaching him, my fear of not being "good enough" to help him reach his goals, and my fear of failure—and eventually something good came of that.

I am not sure what Nick felt about our work, we have since lost touch and I haven't heard from him in many years. I do hope he is as grateful for our time together as I am.

I am thankful for the time we spent together and the success Nick found during our two years as trainer and trainee. He has many decades ahead he can enjoy. I hope I left him with an ongoing reminder of all that he is capable of doing throughout his life.

Most importantly, he no longer sits on a bench in a school yard, laboring to breathe while feeling fat and worthless. There is now promise in his future. And I am grateful for that.

Fear and faith often perform a delicate dance together. We use one to hurt ourselves, and one to restore ourselves. Nick and his family learned that fear of the unknown would be overcome by the faith that there is still a place for them in the world.

They learned that together they could not just survive, but thrive. Years of their lives were spent fearing that their choices would leave them unchanged and disconnected. Their faith in themselves and each other proved that was enough, and they, too, could make a difference in the world.

To my surprise and delight, Nick's mom took it upon herself to make big changes, too. She returned to school and trained for a profession that would allow her to get a higher-paying job. She found a faith in herself that she had never uncovered before, and she realized that our perception of ourselves, when used in a positive way, can be transferred to other parts of our lives.

I learned so much from Nick but my next client who I also worked with for many years would teach me so much more.

Erica did not grow up the same way Nick did, but shared a part of his same journey. She struggled in her life with wanting to lose weight and finding a place in which she could be herself. It would take her until much later in life to realize the full value of her weight loss and the confidence such an achievement would bring to her.

That was the moment when she realized for the first time what being a true champion means. Her story exemplifies how fear of failure can be turned into hope and triumph.

Chapter Two
Erica

Over my years of training, I have witnessed patterns in the types of people who come to me for help. People pleasers and peacekeepers seem to be the ones who suffer most and are often caught in the crosshairs of life. They take on the responsibility of taking care of others (even if no one asked them) and end up leaving nothing for themselves.

Wives, mothers, and caretakers often fall into this category. Fear of hurting others or not being there to support them can cause a person to devote all of their time and energy to others. Unfortunately, the stress that accompanies this fear can create dissatisfaction with their bodies, ultimately leading to obesity and/or weight issues.

It's difficult to ask someone when they will decide to put themselves first. I know in my experience if you don't take care of yourself first, there is seldom anything left for anyone else.

We tend to get it backwards—others first; ourselves last.

Being brave means you *will* put yourself first, and nothing will stop you from reaching your goals. That doesn't mean you don't feed your kids to get to the gym, but it does mean don't skip your workout because of your kids. Find a balance between the two so that no one suffers, especially you.

Yet, so many women take care of others first and then wonder after the years fly by—what happened? Why can't I get my life back and have a body that makes me happy?

I wish I could convince today's younger women to understand the importance of beginning with themselves first. I seldom have a chance to work with younger women due to the circles I travel in, but I do have one particular client that stands out.

Erica and I first met when she left esthetics school and had opened a small facial business in a local downtown building. Though only in her twenties, she had a relatively large body, and I could tell by talking with her that she didn't feel positive about her size.

She dressed well, but in clothes that seemed to hide her frame in order to disguise her weight. I assumed that in her beauty business, as in the field of fitness, people were constantly sizing her up, judging her for how she looked. I know for me it's an occupational hazard.

Attending parties can be a real challenge. Not only do I find people stare at what I'm eating, they want to spend the evening talking about food, health, and debating the pros and cons of the latest trends. It can make a party-lover like me want to stay home and watch TV.

I can tell you honestly, it's a myth that we trainers always "eat clean" and bench press for hours. The truth is, we eat cupcakes and whine about working out just like everyone else.

The fear we share with any business is that our clients may find out we are human. In my early years, I recall going to a restaurant and worrying that a client might see me order something I shouldn't be eating. After a while, I gave up that foolish notion. I needed to be real.

I was letting my fear of being "found out" override my faith in my ability to do the work I was trained to do. How crazy is that?

That same fear I experienced was part of Erica's problem—potential clients thinking she should have beautiful skin and a svelte frame.

She was pretty. The first time I saw her, I thought she was beautiful, but seemed trapped in an outsized body. If only her body could match her amazing spirit and stunning face, I thought. It's an accomplishment difficult for many. She had an internal beauty as well that came from a helping, caring spirit; a people pleaser at heart.

Our initial conversation was about what she could do for me and how she could help me improve my skin to keep me looking and feeling my best. While I was flattered and excited that she wanted to help me, I wondered if anyone had taken the same interest in helping her. Being brave enough to ask for help was probably scary for her.

Then I realized that she has the ability to help me keep my skin looking younger while I have the power to help her better fit inside her skin. Maybe I could convince her we could help each other.

At the time, I was an inexperienced trainer and wanted to work with anyone willing to expend effort. I couldn't tell how serious Erica was. Would she constantly cancel appointments or chronically show up late? Would she make excuses about why she needed a break and would I end up training her under less-than-ideal circumstances?

Today, after twenty years of training, I am pretty good at breaking up with the clients who fail to follow through. But Erica was unknown.

Then she said something I will never forget.

'If you say you're fat, that's what people remember about you. That's all they see.'

It gave me pause. I thought long and hard about her statement. I knew words have real power, and perceptions help create the story we tell about ourselves. When you suggest something negative to someone with your words, you are handing them keys to unlock the insecurities we all have inside us. And that becomes part of their story, too.

Facial after facial, we talked about fitness boot camps and the new diets she had tried. But week after week, very little seemed to change. She signed up for Weight Watchers and said she hoped to change her life.

As I came to know Erica better, I learned more about how her narrative was created. Her mother, she said, was bold, brave, and outspoken, sometimes saying things so brazen, everyone grew uncomfortable.

'My mother,' she explained, 'says what everyone's thinking, but isn't brave enough to say out loud. I think she is made of cast iron. Her words fall like a hammer. I have no doubt that's one of the reasons I became a people pleaser. I knew people were uncomfortable with being confronted, as I had seen my mother do so many times, while I wanted everyone to feel good and be happy.'

Erica, like so many, believed her behavior and words could influence the happiness of others. She hoped by making people feel better that she could change the trajectory of their lives, when in reality, the only person we can truly create happiness for is ourselves.

Her choice to stay in the background and make sure other people feel comfortable is what had led to her overeating. She put her feelings out of sight by retreating to her favorite food, a behavior we often use to numb the fear that if we are open, honest, and what some perceive as "selfish" by tending to our own needs, we are letting everyone down.

We learn powerful things, both good and bad, from our families; things that help us become either functional or dysfunctional.

Erica didn't date at all in high school because she said she felt self-conscious and uncomfortable in her skin. She had her first boyfriend at seventeen, and after dating for six years, they married. She would often reflect back on her failed marriage as an extension of her years growing up.

She sensed her future husband might not be the best choice for her, but he loved her, and she said she needed that above all else.

As a natural peacemaker, she overlooked the things he did that bothered her, along with harboring a fear that this was as good as it gets. This theme is far more common than it should be. Settling for the status quo, and the compromise that follows, can start the demise of both a marriage and the confidence it takes to change.

It can be conscious or unconscious, with damaging results either way. She confided that he was not supportive of her plans to make healthy changes.

By now, she had agreed to work with me, and seemed truly committed. She had already lost about sixty pounds on Weight Watchers, but wanted to get involved in a new phase that involved slow but steady progress.

She showed up on time, ready and willing to do the hard workouts. She also became meticulous about her eating, which made my job a lot easier. I was proud of her work ethic and told her each time I saw her that she was making great strides. Then she confided in me that there was a problem at home.

Her husband wasn't excited about the body his new wife was creating. He liked the one she had in high school, the one that kept her in the comfort zone of being the peacemaker. The new body came with a little more sass, and this did not sit well with him.

I explained to her we get the kind of love we think we deserve. When we decide we want more and go after it, not everyone is happy for us. The fears of our loved ones often stem from the very poison we create.

They want us to remain the same, even if change is inevitable, and as we want more, the divide grows. Lives begin to split apart. When we want better versions of ourselves, the clash is sometimes too difficult to overcome.

Nonetheless, Erica chose to dig deeper, to reach for her own brave, knowing that in the end her relationship might all fall apart.

There were stops and starts, and times when—despite her hard work—her body did not want to cooperate. As is true for many of us, the scale was not her friend. What she needed was the full support of her spouse.

Though she continued working out with me sporadically, she also decided to do whatever it took to keep the peace at home. She made sure her husband had the dinners he liked on the table, skipping the gym to spend time with him, even if he was only watching TV. This led to setbacks in her weight loss success.

She was more intent on not drawing attention away from him, not yet comprehending that pleasing people can easily become a full-time job. She also noticed because she didn't talk about her weight (her mother advised her not to) very few people commented or noticed her weight loss until she had dropped another thirty pounds.

By then, her photos began to look different. Reflecting back, she said, 'I couldn't believe how big I was then. I guess I was hiding under the weight.'

This, I told her, is how real change happens, through insights that become a power for change to occur. Shedding what you don't need, to get to the person you want to see and be, is the recipe for success.

Erica's marriage took five years to fail, happening only when she resolved to stay on course to become healthier. She wanted a better version of her earlier self. She wanted— for a change—to put herself first.

She often spoke tearfully, with frustration and fear that her marriage had begun to feel like a prison rather than a refuge. Yet she persevered in making the necessary changes to better herself. I believe it's when she started gaining strength through our workouts that she realized the strength and abilities she actually possessed.

Only then could she step out of her comfort zone to make the hard decisions that led to a new direction.

Erica began lifting heavy weights and getting stronger. In my gym downstairs—what I refer to as "the Vault"—she emitted loud noises as she did a workout that sounded as though she was dying. But in fact, she was coming back to life.

Strength training is difficult and takes hard work over time to get sufficient results, which is why so many give up. Erica was not afraid of hard work. She did the work and did it well.

She added three spin classes a week at her local gym, and began a stricter eating regimen.

I have learned one of my favorite discipline tricks from Erica. She told me that when she gets home and wants to get out of her work uniform, she puts on her tightest pants so that she has no room to fill her belly with junk.

It was an ideal trick that I still use to help me avoid eating at night. Erica became my motivation in other ways as well. She helped me stay focused by her sheer determination and her desire to be better. And she has kept my skin in great shape!

We continue to work together three times a week. She has started over many times, but has maintained her weight loss and strives to lose more. She now appreciates her body and how she looks, and is still working like a beast to keep the weight off.

She found a voice that feels good for her and is not as afraid to tell people what she thinks or needs. With a new love in her life, she is beginning to find a new healthy, the inner healthy, that will last.

Like many of us, she has known the fear that if we become who we want to become, people won't always like us, accept us, or support our change. It is true that some people want to stifle success and keep us in our place. But the freedom to be who we truly are is powerful, and may be just what we need.

Her brave, as it turns out, was bigger than either of us could have imagined.

Sometimes in your life a pivotal question arises: How big is *your* brave in achieving your dreams? If we seek what we want in life first, the right people and things that are right for us can find us instead.

As a trainer, I see divorce used as a motivator for some to lose weight and get in shape. But sometimes, hidden problems arise in a so-called "happy" marriage because of life changes, and the confidence that comes with them.

Some people are afraid of the responsibility that can come with being thin. It's not only hard work to keep the weight off, but it's also not much fun. Others are afraid that a newfound, sexier body might unleash behaviors they might have trouble controlling.

Erica is beginning to live her best life now, using her newfound body and self-image to encourage others. She still struggles with pleasing people, but has learned to draw stronger, more visible boundaries. She is engaged to a man who loves her and helps her maintain her new-found freedom. He loves her in a way that frees her to continue to evolve.

Finally, she has learned it was only her fear—not her lack of internal strength—that kept her from being brave.

What if we asked the question of our loved ones, "Would you rather I do things that might make you happy, or take care of myself and become a better version of me?"

How would your friends and loved ones respond? Hopefully, you can answer the question with a resounding, "My loved ones want me to be happy *first*".

Being brave requires us to put our storyteller to the test, meeting our fears head-on, and challenging what we think people want from us. Often, we find we all want the same things—we want the ones we love to be happy, and we want to be happy, too.

Strength actualized is a great metaphor and is often the way people find their voice. When you lift something heavy and do things you didn't think you could do, it can easily transfer into other parts of your life.

Today, Erica smiles more and feels that she can help others in a meaningful way through her experience. Her fear of losing it all is met by gaining all that she dreamed of having.

She is living her best life and uses her newfound body and soul to encourage others. Her weight loss is her doorway to her best version of herself, along with a chance to constantly challenge herself to keep moving forward.

And she continues to ask: How big is my brave?

Chapter Three
Marie

Fear of the unknown; fear of dying; fear of missing out. These are fears we all share and at some point in our lives will all experience. I often tell my clients that the length of their life and its quality should have equal balance.

But too often, people wait for the right time—kids to leave home, work to slow down, or retirement to begin— before the issue of health and how it relates to quality becomes a goal. Too many of us take our health for granted until we are faced with the prospect of losing it. Once you have compromised your health, the fears you once had can become all too real.

Why wait to get in the best shape of your life until the end of it? Doesn't it make sense that we can't predict death, but we can predict a good outcome through a concentrated effort to improve our health?

Some are presented with a chance to make changes and avert an untimely or premature death only through an impending crisis. Marie was one of those people.

In the summer of 2010, she contacted me through one of my newer fitness programs after a friend had referred her.

She said she had been told by her doctor that if she didn't lose weight, she would die, literally.

Diagnosed with non-alcoholic cirrhosis of the liver, only one thing could reduce the aggression of the disease: lose weight. A silent killer, non-alcoholic cirrhosis can cause permanent liver damage and scarring due to elevations of fat in blood levels that create inflammation and subsequent organ damage. Obesity is a strong indicator of cirrhosis.

According to the National Institutes of Health, obesity rates have doubled in adults and tripled in children during the past decade in the U.S.

Losing weight was imperative, Marie said, as it was among the most important things that could reduce the aggression of the disease.

Similar to many people I meet who have tried everything to drop pounds, Marie had already been to Weight Watchers, weighed and measured her food, exercised, prayed, fasted, and tried all kinds of crazy diets. Nothing worked long-term for her.

I suggested she might be a good candidate for a unique approach to fitness training I had designed years earlier. Called the Telephone Fitness Trainer (TFT) program, it had been utilized successfully for a number of clients (more on this later).

Because I wanted my TFT clients to understand their stories in order for me to better understand their motives, I often asked them to send me an email with the details about how they found themselves in the situation they were in, and what made it difficult for them to keep going.

In Marie's case, I wanted to know her "big why".

I assumed that facing death would be her "big why", but when we talked, I found that death didn't seem to be the biggest force driving her. Yes, her fear of dying played a role, but what she really wanted was success and freedom from the hold her body had over her.

She had placed herself in her own trap, similar to magicians who put themselves in straitjackets and enter a confined space filled with water with only two minutes to escape. Do people who fight the battle of weight feel this way, too? Battling weight loss is different in that the clock has no timer and the struggle can last for years.

I explained to her that it wasn't the short time she would be with me in the gym, but the twenty-three hours she wasn't, which would have the greatest effect on her weight loss.

I also knew the TFT program wasn't for everyone. I am not a medical doctor and although, I deal with some of the same medical issues repeatedly and am familiar with the role health problems play in my training, I don't pretend that I can fix each client who comes to me.

Marie, I soon learned, had a complex medical history. I was not sure if I could help her at all.

Even so, she insisted that we at least meet before we began our weekly phone sessions.

I knew her situation had to be serious if she wanted to meet me in person. How would this work within the constraints of the TFT program? I agreed to the meeting, unclear on what to expect, or what she might expect from me.

On the day we met, Marie arrived with her sweet, elderly mother in tow. Marie stood about five feet six and was clearly overweight. A lovely young woman with a kind smile, she appeared to weigh more than two hundred pounds.

Her disposition was less like a woman in crisis and more like a mom who would have warm cookies waiting for you after school. When she spoke, her speech was punctuated with a soft Southern accent and before long, I tagged her as a people pleaser similar to my earlier client, Erica.

We talked about what had brought her to this point, and what she planned to do about it. If you have diabetes because of obesity, it will kill you over time. If you have hypertension, high blood pressure, or other autoimmune diseases due to obesity, they too will likely get you in the end. Marie was given a chance to change her future by making healthier choices and positive changes in the here and now.

The visit included weighing, measuring, a body fat analysis, and photos, in order to have a baseline of information to begin the process.

At first, Marie didn't want to see her weight numbers, though others I've worked with were actually heavier than she was. But as she stepped off the scales, I told her she was starting from a solid two hundred and thirteen pounds, and losing it would be no small task.

Then she went into detail about her medical history.

For example, she had fought breast cancer twice, losing one breast the first time, and later having the other one removed. She became diabetic following chemo, and she dealt with back problems that included disc fusions and hip pain due to the back issues. She struggled with the same fear that many of us share—what if I fail at losing weight again?

The non-alcoholic cirrhosis, or fatty liver, arrived after all the other physical disorders, with potentially life-threatening effects. You cannot survive without a liver. I thought Marie might be desperate enough to do whatever it took to get in shape. But as my former trainer often said, 'If it were easy, there would be a long line outside my gym.'

I wanted to think that Marie, as well as others who came through my door, truly wanted to make a difference in their lives. But the truth is, it does require a lot of work and not everyone has what it takes to follow through. I've also learned as a trainer that the more caretaking a person does for others, the less likely they are to care for themselves.

I suspected this would prove true of Marie, making me wonder about her eligibility as a successful client. It also didn't help that she was a nurse by profession.

Like Marie, many nurses are the worst about caring for themselves before others—and are often the unhealthiest, despite their many admirable abilities to save lives and nurture others.

There's even a label for this: Caretaker Personality Disorder, identified by Dr. Les Barbanell, a Columbia University graduate and psychologist. Though not everyone agrees this condition is a true mental health illness, it is associated with a similar disorder called "compulsive pleasing disorder".

In 2012, researchers at the University of Maryland's School of Nursing found that fifty-five percent of the 2,103 female nurses they surveyed were obese, citing job stress and the effect of sleep deprivation due to rotating shifts, which interfere with body clocks, in addition to working long, irregular hours.

The American Nurses Association (ANA) has since instigated an initiative called "Healthy Nurse Healthy Nation"™ to endorse the idea that when nurses are healthy, patients benefit as well.

More recently, a 2017 study conducted in the United Kingdom, found that more than one in four nurses are obese, meaning their body mass index was higher than 30 compared to rates within the general population.

Even so, having a nurse nearby is like having a guardian angel. If you've ever been in the hospital, then you know how vital they are to making sure you get the things you need.

Yet, based upon statistical evidence that they tend to ignore their own health, I couldn't help but wonder if they struggle with being able to meet their challenges, or doing enough when faced with great demands? Because their jobs are so vital, is it possible that neglecting their own health is just another sacrifice in the line of duty?

I could only make assumptions about these questions, but during my journey with Marie, she helped me better understand this dichotomy.

I could tell when talking to her that she was vested in her many caretaking roles, but upon meeting her, I could also see the fear in her eyes when I asked if she could do the same caretaking for herself. I suspected she saw that as "selfish". Taking care of yourself first is nowhere within the realm of selfishness, I argued.

Was she worried that things she was "supposed" to be taking care of would suffer? Instead, think about being selfish as a way to be *better* for others. That's because if you take care of yourself first, you have more to give to others.

Many of the female clients I see and deal with are kicking their own rear ends far more than anyone else ever does over these very same questions. Marie was no different.

I said we first needed to change the way she talked to herself and how she saw herself. It's no small task to ask someone to dismantle the perceptions that have allowed them to become stuck. You also have to find ways to inspire them to change their perceptions.

Marie's beliefs—that she must take care of others first—had imprisoned her so the odds were stacked against us.

We would have to fight for every little victory.

I understood her struggle all too well. I, too, wanted to help others and help myself last. I had an inner voice that made my worst enemy look like a comfortable friend. I could turn on myself in a minute.

My first task, I realized, was to lead Marie to a place of love and belonging, altering her perspective of what "selfish" really meant. After hearing about all the people and things she had cared for throughout her life, I felt that getting her to focus on herself would be our biggest challenge.

Her nursing role, I realized, gave her societal permission and authority to care for the sick; her church gave her permission to care for the needy and the down and out. Her role as a mother gave her permission to care for her children well into adulthood.

Caring for her husband when he retired would give her one more reason to devote herself to others and avoid managing her own health. Watching her own mother take care of others set the chain reaction in motion.

As our weekly phone conversations unfolded, Marie and I reviewed what we had achieved that had actually worked. For example, eating the same breakfast, making her new diet a habit, or having lunch prepared to minimize eating out were goals that she could reasonably achieve.

Challenging herself to explore why she thought she had no value or lacked the ability to take care of herself was much tougher. Successful weight loss, I said, can be a long-term struggle between doing for yourself, and doing for others—an all-out street fight between you and what lies within you. Marie agreed and committed to working on that change.

I used the airline analogy to explain the importance of self-care: as instructed by the flight attendants, you must place your own oxygen mask on first before you can help others. It makes sense in theory, but for many, it feels foreign and somehow "wrong" when we put it into practice.

How dare you leave the house an hour earlier in the a.m. to work out while your husband and children make their own breakfast, fix your own healthy meal while others cook what they like best, or train for a marathon and ask someone else to pick up your child from school!

My kids can make their lunch, but that my husband cannot make his own dinner just seemed silly to me. I have yet to have a male client explain that he can't work out because his wife needs breakfast on the table before she can start her day. Traditional or not, caring for yourself is imperative to your own good health.

Marie learned this important lesson one small step at a time. In her case, she was fortunate to have a supportive husband and family. Even her elderly mother, who had attended our first meeting, made an attempt to be supportive by not having the sweets and goodies she normally provided when her daughter came to see her.

But could Marie overcome her fears over the long haul?

Spiritual catalyst Teal Swan, who is an author and supporter of the natural health movement, says, "We do not fear the unknown. We fear what we think about the unknown."

Fear is something we all must face in our lives, sometimes daily, making it feel like we are experiencing it in slow motion. I had my own fears while working with Marie. Would I be the right trainer? Would I be able to help her? What if she fails? What if I fail at helping her and her health takes a nosedive?

Throughout our sessions, Marie spoke to me in detail about how she struggled to keep her feelings from getting locked inside her. She was also honest about her food challenges, which meant we needed to continue with a workable plan.

It took more than four years for her to lose sixty pounds and keep it off. But her fear and wrong perceptions about herself had kept her in a prison of her own making for decades prior. So we both understood it would take some time to break down old lies and old walls that were built as a result of those wrong perceptions.

Sometimes, as Marie learned, the weight loss journey isn't about the fat you carry on the outside—it's about the weight you've collected on the inside, and your inability or refusal to get it down. There is only one prescription that can help to heal, and that prescription is to take care of yourself first.

Self-care is not selfish. It's vital to everything we do.

Marie not only showed me how big her brave really was, but she also trusted me to help her and trusted herself to do the work. Since then, she has maintained the majority of her weight loss and continues her journey with new vision and direction.

Perhaps more importantly, she proved that helping others doesn't have to be done at the sacrifice of your own well-being.

Not a bad result for a committed, people-pleasing caretaker like Marie. Or, as she would put it, 'I guess I got my brave on just in time.'

Chapter Four
Finding My Place Through Telephone Fitness Training

I have always been curious about human behavior. When I began fitness training, I knew from my own experience it was an emotional journey as well as a physical one. When you don't feel like yourself, or know you can eat better or exercise more, you beat yourself up with words that can have damaging power.

It's tough to test this theory because the fitness industry makes money on selling supplements, diet books, and gym memberships rather than the power of positive thinking.

But we know from the work of Marisa Peer, an English nutritionist, best-selling author, hypnotherapist, and fitness instructor, that you can change your life with powerful, positive words. Peer has spent decades helping people realize *the way they speak to themselves* can make all the difference in achieving their success.

I, too, wanted to be a therapist, beginning my journey in 1994 at the University of Maryland. I took twelve graduate hours in family therapy and hoped to become a private counselor. Many of my classes dealt with traditional talk therapy, and I realized then I wasn't much into talking about problems—I was more interested in solving them.

Though I decided instead to finish my masters in human resources, I never abandoned my fascination with and exploration of how our words and emotions can affect all aspects of our lives, including our weight loss success.

I witnessed clients show up with full determination and a week later, struggle to find the motivation needed to get to the gym. I wondered why clients would say they were all in, but later found out that was only until their favorite restaurant offered a special, or the wine they loved, showed up on the table.

Why did people frequently sabotage themselves after their initial success? Was it really all about diet and exercise—or was it more?

Do the mindset and the words we use to describe ourselves and our disposition have more to do with our results than we first thought? That was something I thought hard about in order to find new ways to approach my clients.

But I had to undergo changes and challenges of my own before I could do anything about it. The challenges began when I moved to a different city.

The move to Asheville, North Carolina, in 2003 turned into a setback for my fitness business. I had been in Raleigh two years, where teaching and training were much easier, given the number of gyms all over the city. Asheville was different in that it was caught in what felt like a time warp at that period in its growth (it has since become a hip tourist town).

For example, "trendy" aerobics classes had come and gone in the bigger cities, but were still thriving in this small mountain town.

Some of the newer things I had learned came across as foreign to the fitness people I met, making me feel even more out of place. The TRX, a strap used for training anywhere with handles and a carabiner; it could hook to a tree or a door jam and you were able to use it to work out anywhere (hence the name TRX—training anywhere). It had been in use for a couple of years nationwide, but it took another five years to become a "hit" in Asheville.

I had hoped my fitness training business would be easy to reestablish, but even that was an obstacle to overcome. Asheville, at the time, with a population less than 100,000 and only forty-five square miles in size, wasn't big, and its population was spread out. The county, Buncombe, extended more than six hundred square miles, so it often felt as if I were driving from one end of the world to the other.

I selected a gym site located in the southern end of town, but found myself getting requests from all over the county for training through email, phone calls, or referrals from friends or their family members. Closer to home, business was proving adequate, but it was still a financial struggle.

Marketing yourself is always a challenge with a small business, but as a fitness trainer in the early 2000s, it was difficult to find business because so many of my referrals were word of mouth. This was on the cusp of social media, before Facebook, Twitter, LinkedIn, blogs, and podcasts became standard ways to network.

That meant that getting referrals required getting to know people, then asking them to recommend you to others.

In other words, your training business at that time required a direct sell.

Following my arrival in Asheville, I had the desire to do more training, yet I still couldn't figure out how to be in all places at once, or how to create more time. Granted, I had some great clients and many of them helped me gain more business. But I knew the model I was using would eventually create a dilemma; there would be more clients than my time allowed me to handle.

By 2007, I was working with a client who knew a large number of people. She invited me to a party at her home. I love going to parties, especially to meet people who don't know what I do for a living.

That's because two things happen at parties where I am introduced as a fitness trainer: I end up listening to confessionals about how the person knows what to do but they just don't do it, and why they think that they don't. Or I hear them swear "I never eat like this".

It's tough when they think as a trainer you can be superhuman and say no to the fancy cakes or yummy food out at a party. After they confess about their own shortcomings, they proceed to watch to see what I eat. By the end of the party as the yummy treats are disappearing, I tend to partake in none because someone is usually watching me. Therefore, my having a "good time" is limited by my business concerns.

Think about it: if they discover I am as human as they are, how would I ever be able to keep clients or find new ones? Though my assumptions might be off base, watching people is part of what I do for a living. A good fitness trainer must be able to read people, determine what they are saying about themselves, and decide who is serious about taking care of themselves or who just wants to blow smoke up the trainer's gym skirt.

On the other hand, I try hard not to treat everyone like a potential client, especially at parties, where most people just want to relax.

For this particular party during the Christmas holidays, I promised I would come if no one would discuss fitness. Also, I wanted to eat chocolate without being indicted. But like all cordial parties, the word was out. Calorie counting and long lists of things people attempt to do in order to become healthy soon became their favorite topics.

It seemed that in every social circle in which I entered the discussion, the subject fell back into eating, exercise, and weight loss. This time, however, I got into a conversation with a young lady who said, 'Jolene, if you would just tell me what to do and then call and check on me, I know I could be successful at follow-through.'

A light bulb turned on. *Why not*, I thought. *What a great business model and what a great way to help more people without adding more travel, more expense, and more equipment!*

In the spring of 2008, I began a trial run of a program I would later call the Telephone Fitness Trainer (TFT). I invited thirty of my closest friends, including people I thought would benefit most from this approach. The first month was strictly a test run to figure out how the business model would work.

There was only one problem. I'm not a big fan of talking on the phone. I prefer texting, or keeping my phone calls short and sweet. In fact, I would much rather talk to someone in person than chat with them on the phone. With that hurdle in mind, I had to figure out a way to keep phone calls brief and concise, but effective.

However, the first couple of weeks consisted of getting to know each person and their stories. Yes, that meant long talks on the phone, and often the long version of what was supposed to be a short story.

I heard "to make a long story short" at least a thousand times. Each conversation was different in the details, but the bottom line was always the same: they didn't know how they let themselves get so far off track, and they needed someone to help redirect them.

It felt like a good way to begin. But as the weeks went by, the business began to bleed. The program included a free session to start. That soon evolved into my time was also free. In addition, I learned that people love to talk about themselves, making their short stories longer than needed.

I discovered that everyone has a theory about how they got to where they were, but no one has a cure. I learned that excuses can sound silly and time can slip by for many people. And before long, I learned I would never make any money if I didn't figure out how to help people put their stories into what resembled CliffNotes.

Finally, I designed a three-question approach and a plan for the time frame I would be working with them. The three questions were:

1) What did you do this week that worked?
2) What did you do this week that didn't work?
3) What will you do next week to maintain or change those two things?

I followed up with: How can I help you be successful?

I allowed the client to talk about five minutes for each question before I encouraged them to move on. I began to get really good at this, and it almost became a game to see if I could keep the call to a maximum of fifteen minutes.

I found that by asking my clients brief questions and getting brief answers, it was no longer necessary for them to provide long monologues about why they were or were not successful. In turn, clients were getting better at sticking to the facts and not letting white noise or excuses keep them from doing better. It was a win-win for all.

Dramatic narrative, I concluded, is a distraction that keeps people stuck.

People have all kinds of reasons for not losing weight or getting in shape, but the truth is it really doesn't matter *why* you don't know; you just need to *do* it.

I also found that with my new line of questioning, clients could think about their answers in advance of the call, which helped them discover their own solutions to a targeted problem. For example, when I asked, 'What did you do this week that worked?' the answer might be zeroing in on a behavior they had used to start their week.

Did that behavior carry through all week, from one week to the next? Did it help them or hinder them from reaching their goal?

A few clients still required more time on the phone than I had anticipated, but I learned not to finish their sentences, which would have limited more elaboration on their part. I stopped trying to figure them out and just listened more. This active listening approach helped me lead them to more personal solutions, rather than a rehashing of the problem.

It wasn't an easy transition, and it didn't always go smoothly. For example, I was, at times, left wondering if they had saved all their words for their single, scheduled call.

One client would relay the illnesses and hospitalizations of everyone she knew. Every call seemed to include doctor visits and medication. Even then, I knew it was important to stay present and really listen.

As the TFT program grew, I began getting clients from all over the world. I worked with a woman from South Africa who was referred to me by another TFT client. My South African client and I would talk by Skype, planning her workouts, her eating plans, and overcoming her obstacles.

I was on a huge learning curve, as I knew nothing about the metric system or dietary details on the South African side of the world. In turn, she taught me about dishes like potjiekos, a traditional stew, and Mealie, a coarse flour used in numerous African recipes.

But what became more evident than the dietary and fitness needs of the clients, was their deep desire to be encouraged. I often found that clients felt isolated, unable to connect to either their successes or failures, as well as to their individual needs.

Some would mention to their spouse or partner they wanted to lose weight and would get the eye roll, which led to a lack of self-confidence. In those cases, they simply needed someone to validate their efforts.

When clients would say, "I feel like you're my cheerleader", I felt that way, too. I found that many took this long, lonely journey to get healthy burdened with the weight of past attempts. There was poison in their perception that dieting was the magic, rather than how better eating habits can fold into your life. Their fear was that if they didn't follow the rules, they wouldn't be successful.

Most weight-loss programs instruct you how to start and what the finish will look like, but few help to explain the hills and valleys encountered along the way. I knew that clients needed to hear the truth that it's a tough process, but the tough part wasn't following the diet or completing the exercise plans.

It was finding out why you don't want to put yourself first or even why you don't feel you are good enough to experience the success of reaching your goals. They needed help in finding their brave, and help in determining how big it could turn out to be.

In all the books I've read on fitness and diets, never have I accurately described the roller coaster ride of weight loss in a realistic way. In truth, as you progress, it's very possible you might want to punch your husband when he says he wants to lose weight, and then, like Superman, enters a phone booth and comes out twenty pounds lighter, as though it all happened by magic.

Meanwhile, you're slugging away at calorie counting and deep knee lunges, sweating off one or two pounds at most. It's not fair, is it?

There's also a chance you are going to see someone whose entire body weighs the same as your right leg, and yet this person considers herself "fat". The perception comes from magazines, the media, the music industry, and pop culture in general. It's no wonder our view is skewed, uncertain what is considered fat, and what isn't.

Before you find yourself with a dead body in your trunk and a need for an alibi, understand I've been there, too, hoping all that deprivation will lead to a place of fitness, freedom and body euphoria.

As a Telephone Fitness Trainer, I walked my clients through this process, instructing them it's not just what they do in the moment that makes them successful—it's that they must keep doing it even when they no longer want to. They must hang on when they really want to hang it up. As a result, I've had some of the same clients for years; clients who tell me accountability is the main reason they signed up, and the main reason they stayed.

I've been blessed with meeting some amazing people in my program. Though they come from all occupations—psychiatrist, life coach, homemaker, researcher, Ph.D. doctorate, student, pastor, and engineer—they all have one thing in common: the fear of being unsuccessful.

When you are good at doing your job and are a good human being, but can't yet master weight loss even after repeated tries, it can become a challenge not to fear failure. I am grateful for the confidence I was able to provide, and the confidence they gave me in return.

Along the way, one of the hardest lessons I had to learn was that I can't help everyone because not everyone is cut out for a phone accountability program. That was a hard reality for me to accept.

In the beginning stages of the TFT program, I took on fifteen clients, composed of friends and colleagues I knew, as well as a few clients I needed to reconnect with in an effort to finish what we started. Though I didn't charge a fee for these repeat customers, I required everyone who participated to agree that I could use their data and their photos.

I did this because people often have a distorted view of how they look. Just think about some of the outfits you've seen people wear that perhaps they shouldn't have. Pictures in the TFT program are taken from the front view, the side, and the back.

I did make concessions for those who lived alone with no one to take their photos, or were really uncomfortable with the whole idea, but I still required at least one captured picture so that clients could see how they changed as they lost weight. Clients are so focused on the scale, they forget to notice how their overall appearance changes.

Those who refused to have photos taken were not eligible clients for the Telephone Fitness Program. At first, I was willing to overlook their refusals but soon learned that by not cooperating, they almost guaranteed an unsuccessful outcome. Others would avoid phone calls, or refuse to answer my questions about sticking to a prescribed schedule.

If I asked these particular clients to call me on their schedule, that didn't work either. Bottom line: some people were not a good fit for the TFT program, and if I wanted to truly help them, I would have to be honest and risk the loss of a sale by explaining they were not the right clients in the right place at the right time.

Men, I found, were easier to work with because they didn't want to think about what they had to do—they just wanted to do it. Women, on the other hand, were more like hostage takers. I had to promise something before they would release something. It made me think about the stories we as women make up in our heads to help encourage or defeat ourselves.

Though always unwise to generalize, I did make a note of the gender differences I witnessed through the years.

Women, I concluded, were not as conditioned as men to accept defeat or success in anything they attempted. Yet they could be competitive and critical, with a strong need to elaborate. Women have a gift for words and they aren't afraid to use them. They will justify, defend, dissect, and often talk to death many of their issues.

Men just seem to barrel through, running roughshod over their issues and strong-arming them back into place, while we females like to provide a good story, lots of background, and context that gives meaning to our reasons for doing almost anything.

Granted, success can be tough on women. I think that's why we need the why's and how's of accepting a challenge during our love affair with success or failure. Overthinking and overanalyzing are how we get through it, and what we commonly tend to do.

This insight resulted in a different reaction from me with my women clients. I would "chest bump" them with words, challenge them on their thinking, and finally ask: 'Would you continue this if nothing changed about your weight?'

Sometimes it worked and sometimes it didn't.

It was through these questions I learned that we women could be fickle when it comes to taking care of ourselves. We give up when we don't get the results we want right away, or get angry and choose to embrace who we think we are, rather than who we want to be. We also tend to make an effort to change our bodies about "everything else", while men keep the struggle isolated to the specific tasks necessary to get the job done.

Men seem to solve problems, while women want to try and understand what they are and where they come from. Men can use working out as a place to relieve stress; women sometimes find dealing with gyms, workout clothes, and calories as stressors.

I saw many women vacillate between compliance and success, no matter how small the success, while men just worked the program and kept on trucking. The truth is, if we could do what we need to do regardless of how we feel, we could easily overcome our fear of failure.

I don't recall a single conversation with my male clients that included the statements: "I hate the way I look and feel. This outfit makes me feel like a cow." What I found instead is that men do want to look good (meaning younger), but it's in an effort to avoid turning into an "old man".

Regardless of these generalizations, everyone I worked with who was successful in the TFT program shared the trait of hard work. Whether you are male or female, there is no way to deny hard work is required, and no matter what your excuse, you must be ready for the journey.

As a Telephone Fitness Trainer, I had a special gift to share. I was able to cultivate a level of trust and confidence with my clients, ultimately learning more about them and their challenges. I could hear in their voices what was going on inside them as I began to explore some of the issues they faced, and how to help them, without becoming their "counselor".

If I heard disappointment in my client's voice and followed up with questions, I might discover they had been let go from their jobs or were facing tough financial hurdles. These setbacks or obstacles affected progress, so it was important to give it attention while not taking away from the goal of getting them healthier and feeling better.

All setbacks, I told my clients, were simply a test. If you knew where you wanted to go and what success looked like, then these obstacles in your path could be turned into opportunities.

I had learned this myself while going through a separation and pending divorce, two moves to two different homes in a short span of time, training for an Ironman competition, and caring for two children while trying to create and maintain income through my fitness business.

The advice I was dispensing was the valuable tool I used to overcome my own challenges.

The TFT program also helped me to see that problems are solved by one step at a time. Each week, whether a client needed to lose ten pounds or a hundred pounds, we set goals and only worked on the reachable goals for that week.

The next week, the client would review goal accomplishment and set new goals. It was walking before running, or the difference between training for a marathon and training for a sprint. Like the age-old riddle: *How do you eat an elephant? Answer: One bite at a time*, we took one day at a time and one step at a time; our goals measured by consistency.

It was understood that everyone would experience setbacks and successes. The trick for me was helping people see both setbacks and successes as incentives toward the end goal.

I loved creating the TFT program and wanted to grow it by increasing the number of trainers and clients. At its peak, I had five trainers who worked with a small number of clients. One of my large corporate clients believed in the program so much they offered to pay for their employees to work with me for an entire year. Seventy-five percent of the program cost was paid for by the company.

My ultimate goal with the Telephone Fitness Trainer program was to have one in every state, possibly all over the world, because I think everyone should have access to a trainer.

Fitness trainers most often get into the business to help people and are simply limited to the number of people they can help by the hours in the day. The TFT program gives them the freedom to help others and not be limited by the hours in a day, or the four walls they train in.

I also feel the model provided two important benefits: knowledge and independence. Many of the people I meet and train insist they know what to do—they just don't do it. But when we get into the actual training, I find they really don't know a lot. Much of what they think they know about fitness is derived from the Internet or through secondhand information.

Once they know exactly what to do, they can set up their own schedules on their timelines. The independence and freedom the program allowed was a huge draw for many people. My program gave people permission and the tools to learn about their own body.

I wanted them to make informed decisions on what they should be doing and what they should avoid, what they wanted to eat, and what they could commit to relative to their lifestyles. I wanted them to write their own better body blueprint, specific enough so they had the right tools to continue or to start over at any point.

Early in 2013, I was called by a wonderful angel from Maricopa County, Arizona, to help with an insurance program, offering TFT for Medicare and Medicaid clients. I was thrilled to think I might be helping people in challenging situations.

The goal was to provide wellness assistance to those who were living far from larger cities, and where many didn't have gyms or local weight loss centers in which to work out. I was elated to be chosen for this task and learned that this lady found my site and program online. As we began talking through the details, I discovered I would be committing to work with a very large group of people.

But I was not deterred.

I set about getting the right number of trainers in place and began making plans to drink from the fire hydrant. This was a huge opportunity, and once we made the commitment, it would be a great way to learn about new demographics and possibly begin helping people all over the country.

The woman in Arizona I was working with said she would send over the legal documents for my review and asked that I have my "legal department" go over them. I was in my car on a rainy afternoon as we talked, and I remember staring into my empty back seat from the rear-view mirror. *There's my legal department*, I thought.

'Right,' I said, full of confidence. 'I'll send it over right away.'

Throughout the next year, as I worked the contract, I came into contact with many different people who had needs I had never imagined. A few just needed someone to talk to. One woman had a fear of going outside, so when we designed her workout, it was composed of literally walking around her living room as she counted the seventy-four steps she would need to take up to five times a day as part of her fitness routine.

Some of the clients suffered from mental illnesses, and my primary job working with them was just to encourage them while doing no harm. A few talked about suicide, and for them all I could do was try talking "life" back into their circumstances. During those times, it occurred to me that I might be in over my head. I was not, after all, a mental health counselor, so I did my best to keep things as basic for them as possible.

Once the year-long contract was over, I realized I should work on the business growth model to minimize over-selling and avoid getting myself into a similar, overwhelming situation.

In truth, I was relieved when it was over because I felt these special clients were not a good fit for the TFT and what I could offer them.

At the same time, I learned a great deal about how to create and provide a better program for a wide range of clients. I had altered my perception of my own skill set during this process, concluding that I could not be all things to all people.

I remain grateful for the opportunities my time with the state of Arizona gave me.

Today, the Telephone Fitness Trainer program remains a viable vision with the intent of helping a large number of people.

Although, I have since had to put the program on a temporary hold for now, I have developed a training program for trainers and hope to teach them how to be better trainers, being more adept at using the phone instead of the gym.

Someday, if my plans succeed, I hope to look back on the TFT experience and be amazed that it all began one cold winter night at a small Christmas party in Asheville, North Carolina, where I unleashed a business model that ultimately helped those in great need to discover and appreciate their "brave".

Chapter Five
Jessica

For what is your friend that you should seek her with hours to kill? Seek her always with hours to live. For it's in her to fill your need but not your emptiness. And in the sweetness of friendship let there be laughter and sharing of pleasures. For in the dew of little things the heart finds its morning and is refreshed.

– Kahlil Gibran

Growing up an Army brat, meeting lots of people, and making friends all over the world, you begin to realize that each person that comes into your life has something to offer. Each friendship is an opportunity to become a better version of yourself.

I know now that each person I have met in my life has provided me with new eyes to see the world. Jessica was one of those people. The time she spent in my life gave me a chance to examine many things about myself, but also how to observe how others see themselves through adversity. I am eternally grateful for our friendship.

When it came time to prepare for my first bodybuilding competition, staying focused was my singular goal. I had worked exceptionally hard and watched everything I ate. In addition, I taught regular fitness classes at the local gym, so every day was a time challenge.

One week before the competition, I was in the gym getting ready for a class when I spotted a young woman. She was small but buff, working on a machine outside of the group fitness room. As was typical for me when encountering a stranger, I said hello and began to make small talk while waiting for my class to file in.

I asked if she was training for something and she said yes. Turns out, it was the same competition I would compete in within a week. How coincidental was that?

It was fun meeting someone competing in a bodybuilding competition held in our same region, and it turned out that we had several things in common. I had hired a professional trainer, but the emphasis was mostly on weight and weight training, so I didn't get a lot of help with nutrition.

That was our first point of discussion: Was she downing protein shakes? She made a face and said, 'No, protein makes you bloated.'

I began to panic mentally—I was on protein shakes— but kept a straight face and a calm presence.

'Well,' I asked, 'how are the sweet potatoes and oatmeal treating you?'

Again, she gave me a funny look and said, 'I'm eating broccoli, chicken, fish, and eggs, and that's it.'

Now I was in full panic mode. I only had a week to switch to a strict, boring food regimen and hope for the best. During the next week, I obsessed about how bloated I was and wondered how I would recover from that.

When I spotted Jessica at the competition days later, she looked great (so did I), and we shared a laugh over how our conversation about food had plunged me into overdrive. I had almost lost it, I told her.

The "never being enough" theme I carry around with me seemed to rise like a shadow jumping out to startle a foe. My fears about getting on that stage were already on high alert, and I sure didn't need a setback to create more anxiety.

I saw Jessica again in the gym a week or two after we had all returned to our bloated diets and relaxed regimens. She mentioned that if I ever wanted to work out with her that would be great. Well, of course I did! She was in fantastic shape, and finding a woman who worked that hard and pushed that hard was inspiring. No way would I say no.

Soon, we were working out at least once or twice a week. Jessica is barely five feet tall, and on her best day can't weigh much more than a hundred pounds, but make no mistake—she's a *beast*!

We leg pressed until our lower limbs felt like they were falling off, trying to make four hundred pounds our weight goal. Jessica could lift the heaviest weight possible, while I always lagged behind.

We didn't talk much when we worked out together, so we knew little about each other's personal lives except for the basics. I did learn that she was attending physical therapy assistant school and had two children. She had married her high school sweetheart and like me, had a history of engaging in physical fitness.

We were both group fitness trainers, and we were both willing to work like crazy. She pushed me hard, and I would often find myself trying to figure out why someone who weighed so little could outlift and outwork me. Nonetheless, we made a good team.

We discussed our plan to compete in the same bodybuilding competition the following year and how we should get an early start. Prepping for a contest in the beginning can give you a false sense of having plenty of time. Then, as the months fly by, you begin to realize every minute has to count toward training because while you may be good, there are others out there who are always better and stronger.

Throughout our training period, we met whenever our schedules allowed, and worked hard right up until the competition. The workouts were challenging, to the point where we would lament later about how much we hurt and why we did that to ourselves. We still didn't talk much about our personal lives, but I considered the two of us friends.

She was busy with school, and I was busy with training and teaching fitness. During the times we were together, we discussed diets, life in general, and how few people wanted to invite us to parties or listen to us talk about all the hard work it took to look "good".

Soon, the competition day arrived. We each placed well within our categories, hugging our trophies and talking about all the good food we would indulge in after the event. I thanked Jessica for helping to keep me motivated. She had been fun to work out and compete with, but before long, we were back to our regular routines.

She went into her second year at physical therapy assistant school, and I ramped up my business. We still worked out together, but not as much. Though we were still friends, our lives seemed to be taking us in different directions.

Then, one mid-summer day while I was scrolling through Facebook, I saw a post from another friend who said Jessica had been in a serious accident and needed prayers. I called my friend and asked her what had happened. My heart sank as I learned that a car had struck Jessica while she was riding her bike, and that her back was broken.

I was devastated for her. I decided to write an article about Jessica for a local woman's magazine, hoping to generate interest in helping her and her family. In the story, I described my friend and what she had endured:

People say we don't know how strong we are until our strength is all that remains. On 17 July 2011, Jessica Allen began her journey of finding that strength. Jessica, petite but strong, was an avid cyclist and a competitive bodybuilder. Her dimensions seem small on paper, but people watching her train and compete realized that she was anything but small.

She rode her bike to the gym every day and, since the weather was perfect that morning, she headed out. Little did she think that this might be the last bike ride she would ever undertake. Hit by a car from behind, Jessica was thrown into the air and landed on her back. When witnesses stopped to help, she made sure that they did not move her, quick thinking that may have saved her life.

Jessica learned later that she had three broken vertebrae and that her spinal cord was nearly severed. She was rushed to surgery where doctors inserted a rod into her back. Doctors told her that surviving the accident was a miracle and that walking again would, perhaps, be her next miracle. The waiting began.

Jessica grew up in Western North Carolina and met her future husband, David, in the sixth grade. They have two children, a teenager and a young boy. Jessica attended South College for a physical therapy assistant degree and found her passion in working with pediatric patients, helping them learn to walk again after an injury or other medical issues.

No stranger to hard work, Jessica was diagnosed with Crohn's disease (something I had not learned about her) and had to change her way of life in many areas, especially eating. An entirely different diet gave her the drive to stay in top physical condition, a great help after the accident.

After seven days in the local hospital, she was moved to Shepherd Spine Clinic in Atlanta, one of the best places for patients with spinal cord injuries, especially those with additional complications. The clinic accepted patients in their program with a variety of stipulations, most importantly, believing that they would achieve a good outcome. Jessica, fortunately, received that opportunity.

For six weeks, Jessica learned how to get in and out of her wheelchair, how to dress, how to enter a car and exit, and how to navigate life in a wheelchair. Still hopeful of walking again, she used her time in treatment by challenging herself and thinking big. Three weeks after her arrival, doctors told her that, due to the nature of her injuries, she would never walk again.

She refused to accept that fate; Jessica knew what she was capable of accomplishing and refused to make their dire predictions—the end of her story.

After returning home, her real work began. She had no health insurance at the time of the accident, so mounting medical bills and pending insurance claims caused her family additional stress. Jessica now had another challenge: assuring that the medical bills did not claim her family's future.

The Monday following her accident was supposed to have been her first day working at a new clinic with a health insurance package for the family. Tragedy struck before her benefits were in place.

For Jessica, the financial strain was greater than the stress of not walking again. David, her husband, worked with electronic currency devices and owned a software web business. He worked long hours and wanted to finish his degree.

They had invested in Jessica's physical therapy degree at South College the year before to give the family a steady income. In addition, they had finally purchased a first home.

Many have wondered whether the woman responsible for hitting her paid any of the medical bills. Unfortunately, the driver's insurance had a maximum $50,000 liability and that was all that could be awarded. Lawyers could have sued the driver for her personal assets, but Jessica felt that two wrongs do not make a right.

Her new financial challenges included discovering that being in the middle class with some resources prevented her from receiving the help she would have received had she been in a lower income bracket.

As she began to recover, Jessica faced mounting debts and concerns that her once-bright future as a physical therapy assistant had been replaced by dependency on a broken system.

'No one should have to choose between feeding your kids, paying the mortgage, or having a wheelchair that fits properly,' she said. Her reality included harassing phone calls from medical bill collectors, and finally, being dropped by Medicaid, which had helped fill the financial gaps and shortfalls the accident had created.

Jessica's friends joined together and hosted the first annual Champion Challenge, a fitness event that raised about $10,000 to help with the bills. Jessica began working with a local charity to establish a fund for other people experiencing similar hardships, saying she would not be deterred by financial or physical setbacks.

Her husband—her rock—headed up her team. In addition, her father (technically her stepfather, who was there for her from age three) took nine months off from work to accompany her for every exam and rehabilitation appointment.

Since he had a master's degree in Rehabilitation Therapy, he had first-hand expertise and knowledge on treating people suffering traumatic injuries, whether or not paralyzed. He was also part of a team of doctors, nurses, and therapists traveling to hospitals in North Carolina to audit the rehabilitation care that patients similar to Jessica receive.

With this knowledge, he evaluated Jessica's treatment. He knew that her treatment had been some of the best ever; it definitely contributed to her success and would hopefully result in her walking again someday. He continues to be one of the motivating spirits in her life. He has been pivotal in helping Jessica think about this long journey and has helped her keep her positive perspective.

When Jessica heard that she would never walk again, his advice to her was, 'Cry today; cry as much as you need to because you have earned the right to cry. But, after today, you cannot cry anymore because you need every ounce of energy to get better, to heal, and to learn to walk again.

'It is hard to imagine focusing on the half-full part of the glass, rather than the half-empty. You had many wonderful years of using your legs, but the important thing to remember now is that you are still alive with family and friends all around you.'

Jessica must still overcome many hurdles, but she also has years of life to enjoy. She is a fighter with a strong belief in God and a faith that she will overcome this setback. She is more committed than ever to walking again and proving to others that her motto to never give up is truly how she lives.

Inspiring others is a gift Jessica has always had, and she will continue changing her life and the lives of others.

* * *

Jessica was, and remains, my hero. The day after the accident, I went to the hospital to see her. I was shocked to see her covered in bruises and flat on her back. She could hardly move her head. They were keeping her still so the spine would heal.

It was hard to believe our little Mighty Mouse (my pet name for her) was so broken, she didn't know if she would ever walk again. Careful not to state absolutes, doctors wouldn't say she would never walk again, but instead said "it was too early to tell" due to the severity of the injuries.

Jessica had a brave bigger than someone three times her size. It drove her to fight, keep fighting, and would become part of her ongoing battle. Her only deficiency was that in spite of her usual positivity, she at times believed she wasn't big enough and brave enough to overcome this.

She shared with me that she had battled depression in the past and had a family history of psychological challenges. She spoke about her mother's bipolar disorder. Her brother took his own life due to depression. I feared her experiences and fears would be one mountain she might not be able to conquer.

As a physical therapy assistant, she also knew her situation was serious. This would be no ordinary competition between her will and her strength. Instead, this would be a hurdle larger than anything she had experienced. Could she defy her own beliefs about her self-worth and overcome her fears?

In the hospital, I sat next to her and held her hand. All I could say was, 'I am so sorry.' As a friend in these circumstances, you grab at things to say to make it better, knowing if you were the one lying in that bed, nothing could make the fear go away.

I wouldn't have wished this on my worst enemy, but if I could think of anyone who was ready for the journey, it would be Jessica. She was no stranger to work and difficulties, and she would find a way to overcome this latest challenge. Of that, I was certain. And I told her so.

I imagine it is common to lie to your friends when they are bedridden, facing permanent paralysis. You dig deep to put on a brave face when in your heart you know this is the worst situation you have seen in your life to date, and there is no magic wand to make it all go away.

The lie begins with, "This is going to be okay. You will be okay", followed by "You've got this and this can't beat you". You try to be strong for them, but your heart aches knowing no one should ever have to go through this. You want to pull out a warm blanket instead, cover them up, and tell them a story with a happy ending.

You close your eyes tight and wish it all away. In your heart, you think "that could have been me", and you wonder what it would really take to overcome, knowing all along a secret part of you is glad it wasn't you. You keep secret the fear that you have for them, covered with a brave face, topped with dinners and gifts you drop off at their house.

But I had bigger questions. Was this something that happened to her or for her? Could she take on the demons of the past and make this story a victory story, or would her history be too great to change the outcome? Would she play small and fear the greatness waiting for her?

Adversity isn't always our enemy. It can be our teacher. I knew from my experience before this accident that Jessica struggled with the belief that she was good enough, therefore always downplaying her success. Would she have the courage to step into the shoes she knew she could fill? How big would her brave be?

David, Jessica's husband, is the other hero in this story. While in the hospital, Jessica told him if he wanted to leave her because she would be no good to him, he could. She told him it was her fault she had been hit and she would now live with the consequences.

In response, David called a pastor to the hospital and had him renew their wedding vows. David explained he got hit by the car that day, too. He was paralyzed in the worst way because there was nothing he could do but watch his wife suffer. He couldn't fix it, so he had to bear the burden of his inability to make it better.

David would, too, face some demons from the past. I can only guess they swirl around while we protect the ones we love and letting things happen and why these things happen? It was classic bad things happening to good people.

As the bills mounted, David took on more and more work and fought like hell for Jessica. He loved her, and despite a normal amount of anger over the accident, I think he was the strongest of us all. He showed us what real valor and real love looked like.

Jessica taught me many things, too; so many I could write a book simply titled "What Jessica Taught Me", but the best part of our time as friends was yet to come.

Jessica had worked hard on a comeback to see if she could walk on crutches unassisted. The pool at the therapy center was the site where this would happen. She called and asked if I could be there on the day she planned to take her first step in the water, thereby turning the doctors' predictions into a whole different story. I wouldn't have missed it for the world.

It was Veterans Day and the kids were out of school, allowing me more time since I could avoid their drop-offs and pick-ups. As we waited in the pool area, Jessica confided that she was terrified. She had no idea if she would be able to walk, and even more frightening to her was the knowledge that the first step might determine the rest of her life.

If that first step in the pool didn't happen, she said, she would be confined to a wheelchair for the rest of her life. Can you imagine your whole life hinging on a first step?

But then…aren't we all afraid of the first step, both good and bad in anything we do?

What happens after that first step? Will we walk or run? I knew that day by the pool, whether Jessica was able to take that first step or not, she would never give up. And I knew there was real victory in trying.

Watching her, I was convinced she would take that first step. She had willed it to happen, and despite her real fears, her courage would prove even bigger than her fear.

As she rose from the chair in the pool and moved forward, we all cheered and cried, knowing that her day had finally come. Light would finally shine in the dark place from which she had traveled; a place she had fought her way out of, if only for a moment.

***

Today, Jessica remains mostly chair-bound, but continues to compete in wheelchair bodybuilding competitions. She and I talked about the two of us doing an Ironman competition together one day. She works out four to five times a week and maintains a regular physical therapy schedule.

Her hard work paid off when she was selected *Ms. Wheelchair North Carolina* in 2015, traveling across the state telling her story to inspire others.

She also became a physical therapy assistant from her chair, but now works as a trainer with therapy patients individually, inspiring everyone she meets. Each time I see her, I remind her, 'I'm not scared of hard things because of what you have been through,' and that I will never give up because of her.

I know that although I've been brave at times throughout my life, she has fought a greater battle. I am proud to call her my friend and reflect in the light she creates from all she has overcome, and all that she has become as a result of her arduous journey.

I run a few extra miles these days, knowing that if Jessica could do it, she would. I work a little harder when I really want to quit because of Jessica, and I know now that all of us are capable of more than we think is possible. Therefore, I push a little harder, too.

Jessica and I seldom see each other anymore, but I know that our friendship has given me a new perspective and a way to live more deliberately. Through Jessica, I have learned that sometimes our best, bravest step is the first step. This lesson would come home to me repeatedly as I began working with a new set of clients who—despite their own challenges—were willing to risk moving forward, one painful step at a time.

This new set of clients were women who had their own perceptions that required examination, fears and limitations, and reluctance to recognize and appreciate what their collective raw determination and inner power could accomplish.

We had a special place where we came together to discuss these things and so much more. This place and these women were my "Ladies of the Vault".

Chapter Six
The Vault

The middle years for women can be among their most challenging. While men have a midlife crisis, it is often different for females. Men do the iconic things like getting new sports cars or new wives, or both. But for women, we tend to overlook how different and life-changing our middle years can be.

In a woman's early years, if she has children, she is managing their young lives like the human resources department of a family-owned business. Who she is and what she studied in college, as well as her success in life prior to children, can take a back seat to her roles as caregiver, creator, and facilitator, helping her kids reach responsible adulthood.

Many women struggle to have an identity outside of their job as a parent. In some cases that is their sole identity—being a mom. As a fitness trainer and a mother, I have always felt a deep connection and desire to help keep this particular group of women healthy.

They typically put their children and partners first and wait till kids leave home to prioritize their health, which can often be too late. Years can go by and they seem to be lost in the priorities of others, wondering how they got to where they are now.

I felt this same squeeze—how to be a good mom and a healthy woman independent of my role as a mother. While competing, which required being at the gym for six a.m. workouts, I worried that my kids wouldn't be ready when I ran home to drop them at school each morning.

Most of the time, however, they were ready.

I had an idea to create an opportunity for women's independence, believing it would help them become better humans. But I still had to wrestle with the mommy guilt to make space for myself. And I had to figure out how to make my personal goals a reality.

What I really wanted was to operate my own gym.

Most trainers cherish the romantic dream of owning a gym; the type of place people can come to change their lives for the better. While I was no different, I had no idea how tough it would be to open and maintain a successful fitness center while caring for my family.

The harsh reality is that getting paying clients in the door, and keeping them, is a major task, along with covering utility bills, equipment costs, overhead, and all the other expectations and responsibilities that accompany a small business.

Because I lived in a county that was huge, with potential clients widespread, the first order of business was to find a place centrally located. I researched several sites, but the commute was too long for clients to come to me, or me to go to them. Fortunately, we had just sold a small house and moved to a larger home that included a roomy basement.

Why not start there, I thought? It took a couple of years to convince my family this was a good idea, but over time, by purchasing sturdy used equipment, building my client base, and offering moms the convenience of morning classes, the transformation took place. Four women signed on, then another, and another.

It was soon referred to by my clients as "the Vault", a place where all secrets came to life and would never be revealed past those four walls. While working out, moving from one station to the next, we talked of troubled marriages, difficult children, finding our own place to fly, what worked best and least in our lives. Nothing was off-limits. There was only one rule: whatever was said must be kept in the Vault.

It worked out best to limit four people at a time in the Vault, as I could devote more time and attention to each. My job was to facilitate the workout while monitoring the conversations to ensure we were careful not to say things we couldn't take back, or have workouts that were less than effective due to chit-chatting.

Not only did I learn a great deal about these women, but many became close friends with whom I still have a bond today.

Kate was tall and full-figured with a personality that oozed love and concern. With fiery auburn hair and pale skin, it was as though she carried a halo of light wherever she went. A robust woman her entire life, she stood roughly five feet ten and weighed more than two hundred pounds, but she carried it well.

Due to her height and build, she always looked stout and strong rather than heavy and out of shape. She was a pretty woman with a great smile that welcomed everyone she met. She was also that friend and client who could turn a simple shoebox into a magical gift box filled with her homemade goodies; the one who could make blackberry jam from the bush at the end of her driveway for fifty of her closest friends.

Though her laugh filled the room and Kate was a bright addition to the Vault, it was difficult to watch her always put herself last, as though her own needs didn't matter. I also wished that she wasn't judged by a world which too often honors body types and surface appearances over a good heart. Thanks to wrong-headed perceptions in society, a woman who is selfish is too often classified as "bad" while being selfless makes you a better person.

Men work long hours and spend time furthering their career. It is considered admirable. Yet, we learn through trial and error that it is quite the opposite.

Blessed with a happy marriage, Kate lived in the same home she grew up in and retained her childhood relationships with friends who were now well on their way to middle age.

On the flip side, she struggled with many of the same issues we all do—food, body image, and a sense of belonging. Like others I've met in my work, she was among the kindest of people who do so much for others to gain love and acceptance, but don't extend those same virtues to themselves.

She knew and loved everybody, helped others, and always had time to listen or care with a full measure of kindness. But when it came to herself, she never seemed to make the time to tend to her own needs. She had tried every diet on the planet, would yo-yo up and down, and then had to work hard to put on a brave face whenever she gained back the twenty or so pounds she had lost.

To her credit, she laughed at her shortcomings and often made fun of herself before others could make fun of her first. A popular friend, she always showed up for her workout with a list of things that had to be done and people who had to be cared for after she was through with her exercise routine.

The women of the Vault offered each other a glimpse into their lives, but to me, they represented women everywhere. We shared what made us afraid, the fear of being discovered or not having it all together, or worse, not being enough. We dissected our lives and explored what demons we needed to conquer. In the years we worked together, we taught each other many things.

Our bodies might be different sizes, different shapes, and different heights, but the hearts were very similar in all of us. I found we all wanted to love ourselves and to love others in a better way each day.

As their trainer, I learned another valuable lesson. If women were more open and real with one another, perhaps the hidden walls of doubt about our self-worth wouldn't imprison so many of us; erroneous perceptions would not poison us.

Cynthia, another member of the Vault, was special like Kate, but in a different way. She was, in fact, what some might call a little crazy. To me, that meant she was also interesting. Every trainer has at least one of these client types—the one who runs through the door of each session with her hair on fire, mumbling about this or that while she takes her place within the group.

With frazzled, curly hair and a medium build, Cynthia was about five feet seven and no more than ten pounds over her ideal weight. She was in relatively good shape and just wanted to continue her conditioning, though she suffered from the "if only syndrome"; as in: "If only I could lose ten pounds, I'd be happy".

I wondered if people realized the gravity of that statement. I would sometimes respond to Cynthia with, 'If ten pounds is the only thing between you and happiness, shame on you!'

By that, I meant that ten pounds is nothing to lose when happiness is at stake, knowing it was more than the ten pounds that kept them unhappy. Happy or unhappy is just a difference in perspective. Happy is a power that comes from our perceptions; unhappy is a poison.

Cynthia had other self-worth issues as well. According to her version of life, she was often misunderstood, and experienced many disappointments that left her feeling isolated and insecure. She said she had dealt with body image issues her entire life.

Though she was never slim, she still wanted to look like the fashion models she admired. She bemoaned the fact she was always the "medium-sized girl" who could never feel special.

Her husband worked continuously and according to her, was a hustler who made good money, but largely ignored her. Because he was always busy, she felt that he chose his work over her. Her sense of abandonment led to an obsession with food and she needed help, she said, help in filling the emotional void.

Cynthia came to many workouts defeated and obviously frustrated about her life, her body, and ultimately the choices she made. She was trapped by her unworthy perception of herself.

She knew she would never look like the "skinny" moms at school. We all wondered if she secretly wanted to be part of that same moms' group, sipping martinis while gossiping about other moms. Instead, she leaned toward peanut butter and jelly sandwiches, or leftovers from high-calorie food she cooked for the kids, all the while vacillating between three different sizes of clothing.

It seemed she always found a way to deny herself and all her efforts, ending up back at square one, beating herself up in the Vault, hoping we'd all come to her rescue. I frequently found myself reminding Cynthia about her good qualities in order to get her back in the game.

Despite the times she was locked up in her own little world, in which I'd have to explain the exercises repeatedly while the other ladies of the Vault lost patience, Cynthia could be fun to workout with on her better days. In truth, I think she needed constant affirmation. She needed to know she was okay, even if she thought we were lying to her about how she looked.

While there was little wrong with her body, her attitude needed adjustment. In that regard, she was like most of us—a work-in-progress.

Our journey through the Vault was a delicate balance, not just for me, but for all of us. I wanted to make a difference in the lives of these women so they could become successful in their fitness goals, while attempting to find the right combination of personalities, good hearts, a willingness to work hard, and a lot of transparency.

In other words, I wanted to help each of them find their brave in order to help them become the best version of themselves they could be. At the same time, I felt blessed to witness them at their best, and their worst, struggling to evolve as they grew through the process.

Georgia was a wonderful, fun client to work with and joined our group with great ease. She didn't want to lose weight and, frankly, she didn't need to shed pounds. She just wanted to workout in a group and be around people who strived to be better.

She said she loved the atmosphere in the Vault, hoping to be part of something that could have an impact on others. She was tall, about five feet eleven, with dark hair, pretty eyes, and pale skin.

She did have "spots" (her words) on her body, cellulose areas that she disliked. Nonetheless, she was always positive and upbeat, appearing to enjoy whatever workouts we underwent that day. She explained that she wanted to work hard, build muscle, and live longer. I thought she had the right perspective and appreciated that she was always so positive.

The other ladies loved it when Georgia was in our workouts because they all felt she made them more willing to work harder. Unlike the others, Georgia wasn't from the local area.

She had moved to the South from New Jersey and hoped to make new friends.

She worked hard on her eating habits and made sure she was doing the right things by checking in with me, as well as the group, asking questions and comparing her diet to everyone else's.

As she rattled off her organic array of good food and juice sessions, we all wondered why it was so easy for her to eat healthy. She was like the girl in school who was pretty *and* smart.

How fair was that?

Combine the good eating habits with her kind and encouraging nature, and it came as no surprise that everyone secretly wanted to take a shot at her. She was the one woman in the group we could all talk about, as though she had the most incredible perfect life and the perfect body, matched with the perfect attitude. As a result, we secretly wanted to witness her eating a cupcake or a doughnut—no doubt to offset our own shortcomings.

I believe all of us really wanted to be more like Georgia. However, we had too many giant fears to confront. Georgia was so well put together it was difficult to know if she had any fears of her own. I assumed she did because we all do.

Finally, the day came when Georgia admitted to us that her husband had been having an affair. She was lost, not knowing what she would do next. We were shocked to know that everything that shines is not always gold, and our "perfect" Georgia had a life as imperfect as our own.

After her revelation to the group, I realized that Georgia's fear was never being good enough and that her admirable eating habits and religious workout regimen were just her way of trying to avoid failure. Her husband didn't sound like a bad guy, but when men cheat, all women tend to see them as villains. How could a man who had so much decide to find someone else?

That was our burning question within the group.

We were all confused by that, wondering if our lives in all their imperfections were vulnerable to the same condition. Georgia and her husband did try to reconcile and she continued to come to the Vault with a great attitude and a willingness to work, while shrouded in pain that none of us had fully known or understood.

She had successfully juggled her personal life and her workouts, keeping them separate until she could no longer bear the pain alone.

She eventually realized that her fears over her marriage had come true, but that rejection could lead to a new journey to find acceptance in herself. She counted herself lucky to get another chance at love and life, and stayed positive. In the end, she was the type of person that makes us all better people by allowing us to bathe in her positive light.

I knew she would be able to handle whatever obstacles challenged her as she attempted to move forward.

By contrast, Tiffany made me a little nervous. She loved to work out, but would always lift the heaviest weight, do the highest number of reps, and try to outwork everyone in the group. I was nervous because I was sure she would hurt herself—or worse—hurt someone else with her unstoppable energy.

Tiffany was short and stocky with fifteen extra pounds she had hoped to lose for the past decade. She had a lovely face, with auburn hair and green eyes, along with a great wit. She seemed sincere when she came to work out, but her attitude was: the harder she worked, the quicker she could shave off the weight.

That, unfortunately, doesn't always prove true, especially in her case because she had an ongoing love affair with food.

It was clear this affair had been underway for quite some time. She often described food as though it were a Latin lover. Within the up-and-coming town of Asheville, more frequently known as the "Sedona of the South", we are privy to world-class restaurants, making it even more difficult for Tiffany to get past her obsession with great food.

Asheville has also become known as a beer town, rival only to Portland, Oregon, and Philadelphia, Pennsylvania, with microbreweries everywhere. Tiffany knew all of the best places to go, making no apologies for her indulgences.

She hoped that all her hard work would pay off, but as she confided her hopes to the ladies of the Vault, we all listened, knowing she was in big trouble due to her food addiction and easy access to temptation.

There are, by the way, many "Tiffanys" out there. At some point, everyone I've worked with has said, 'I eat healthy. I just need to exercise.'

Exercise is the body and brain collaborating over what you can consume. But you can eat too much of anything, even if it's healthy. More often than not, our body can't keep up with our intake levels, which is why even a "good" diet can give too many calories, resulting in weight gain.

Working out is sometimes like penance after confession, and is done to help us feel better when we make mistakes. Our food and the choices we make are the defining factors in what happens to our bodies. Yes, exercise helps, but without the right fuel, it can't make you stronger.

The body can't help you exercise away bad choices.

Exercise is the energy your body should use up daily, but what you use in order to fuel your engine makes a big difference. I think Tiffany knew, as we all do, that her devotion to food would prove to be too much for her body type. She would have to reduce her intake—cool the affair—or learn to live with the consequences.

Tiffany did well for a month or two and then a big party with friends would prompt her to strategize yet again on how to dissolve the lurking fifteen pounds that were not going away. The party would come and go, and so would Tiffany's desire to take on that challenge and make those necessary, lifelong changes.

She finally said that she was okay with being who she was—even when she clearly was not.

In the Vault, we began as strangers, but over time, in a small space filled with sweat, sometimes tears, our sharing of life's myriad of problems became one of the most wonderful and gratifying things I've ever known. Other women in the Vault said the same.

It has been my experience in the fitness business that people who show commitment, work hard, and don't fall prey to comparing themselves to others, are the most successful at reaching their fitness goals.

Women, in particular, are capable of tearing down even the most confident woman. As referee and parade marshal, I knew it was important that the workouts I set up in the

Vault were reasonable, achievable, and challenging, but not annihilating.

I wanted the women who came through my doors to feel a certain amount of success, to be safe, and to build the bodies they were looking to build, even those who were challenging to work with, or were Doubting Thomases when it came to their own capabilities.

Today, the "Ladies of the Vault" continue with their workout routines, having moved on to other trainers due to individual circumstances. Yet, I will always remember them as a rare breed that enters a gym without ego, bringing only their grit and good intentions. With these folks, their aim is simple: spend time with others, smile, laugh, feel better, and make everyone around them feel better, too, while building stamina and strength.

For that reason, my time with the women of the Vault was magical. From what I have heard since, they felt much the same. In the end, many said that walking through my "vaulted" doors was the best thing they had ever done for themselves. They came seeking a better human body; they left having found a better human spirit.

I am humbled to have been part of their personal journey. It remains a large part of why I continue to do what I do. I think about how blessed I am that I have gotten to know so many people on such an intimate level. This privilege has both changed and sustained me.

***

Dr. Brené Brown, vulnerability researcher and a professor at the University of Houston, offers insight on the anatomy of trust. She says it's the little things that build up to the overlying trust we share with one another.

She refers to the act of trusting someone as "marble jar moments", the things our tribe and friends do for us to allow us to trust them. Small gestures like taking time to listen when a friend is struggling, calling when we know a friend might need a kind word, and being present when a crisis arises are all acts of trust. Her daughter attended school and vowed after a tough school experience with friends to never trust anyone again. Brown explains to her daughter that trust is built as we share stories about ourselves with others. The marbles are added to the jar the more stories one shares with another. Seeing a jar full of marbles allows us to open up and share with one another. Trust is then built through the "marble jar moments" like the moments shared in the vault.

The Vault was a place where marble jar moments happened a lot and they allowed all of us to know we had people who looked out for one another. A safe environment, where acceptance is full and total even when our worst traits are exposed, is critical to changing your life when you are hoping to lose weight or get into shape.

One of the most lasting things I learned from the brave women of the Vault is that the team you end up with matters. Having a good team in the gym helps everyone attempt their personal best.

Sometimes you pick this team; sometimes they pick you. Sometimes they help each other find their way through the poisonous influence of false perceptions; and sometimes they help you find your way to a powerful new way of thinking.

Being brave also means accepting the fact you must put yourself first.

The women of the Vault found their brave by taking the chance that people they loved and cared for could survive without them constantly being present. They continue to work out, continue to face their personal issues, and continue to thrive in a world that tells them they are "selfish" for doing so.

Chapter Seven
Building a Team

Have you ever wondered if our lives have been marked out for us from the beginning of time? Did God know what I would be doing in my life and purposefully put people in my path who would help me get to where I wanted and needed to go?

I believe that each person we meet, who becomes our friend, has a task with the primary purpose of enriching our lives. But how and why do friends play such a role in the growth and development required for us to reach our destination?

Making friends can be a challenge, finding those who make you a better person, even more so. Sometimes it's a matter of being in the right place at the right time. The person you need to help move you to a more evolved place simply shows up.

When we find our brave and begin to act on it, we need the kind of people in our lives who will ask us hard questions, laugh and poke fun at our ideas, challenge us to challenge ourselves, and in the end, comfort us when failure sends us back to start over again.

I consider the people who have walked me through this life as my early team, showing up to help me learn to become braver. Conversely, the fear and faulty perceptions we overcome can be the very things our friends need to find their own brave.

Friendships require a fair amount of sharing who we are (the good, the bad, and the ugly) to get to the best parts of friendship. Being vulnerable is a gift to others while sharing ourselves.

How big is our brave when we ask someone to look past the yucky parts of who we are and just see the good parts? How do we allow others to cheer for us if we don't tell them what we are up against? Friends make the difference in the journey, and give us someone to share in our joys and sorrows.

The people who are on your "team" and how they have contributed to your goals can make the difference between success and failure in both your professional and personal life.

Professionals in the field of personal growth maintain that you are the average of your five closest friends. Relationship experts conclude that you should consider yourself fortunate if you can count five people in your life as close friends. In a sense, they both make a point.

As I write this story, I have come to believe it is *who* you spend your time with that's most important in your journey, not where you're going or what you're doing. Although tasks are important, it's the people in your life that are the most vital part of achieving those goals and becoming who you aim to become.

I've been fortunate to have encountered some amazing people; people who through the power of their personalities and the gifts they brought to me and others, helped guide me to where I am today.

Being a military brat and traveling much of my life, I realized early on that the groups I traveled with and the friends I made were my positive "game changers". But not everyone is so lucky.

Do you recall the story of Gulliver who lands upon an island with the little people called "Lilliputians"? Out of fear, they lash Gulliver to the ground. Their village mentality is a vivid example of why people fear what they do not understand.

Make sure when you begin to build your "team"—those people you surround yourself with—that you choose those most likely to build you up rather than, like Gulliver's fate, restrain you.

Part of my journey as a fitness trainer has been to find people who "get me" and won't tie me down out of fear; people who help me push the brave in order to bring out whatever positive lies within.

Though the people I write about in this chapter are part of my personal team-building story, my actual "team" is bigger than the people I write about because we are the sum of all the people in our lives. In South African, the word "Ubuntu" is a term that translates, "I am because of you". The people I write about in this chapter are my "Ubuntu". I am here because of them.

They are the cornerstones to the house that built *me*.

Jonathan was my first team partner. He was my cousin by marriage and we became friends as well as family. I was sixteen in 1986, and my father would take us to his sister's home to be with her family over the school break in Albuquerque, New Mexico.

Tall and handsome at seventeen, Jonathan was my aunt's stepson from a previous marriage. He had dark brown eyes, a great smile, and seemed shy when we first met. After that first summer, we became pen pals, forging a great friendship that would last for years.

On one of my summer trips to New Mexico, I got a job working part-time at the dry cleaners. After hours, I hung out with Jonathan. He had been sick with strep throat at fifteen but didn't finish his round of antibiotics, which can result in a condition called Streptococcus.

One day on the tennis court, he suffered his first heart attack. It caused a valve to fail, requiring replacement with a pig valve—a common practice in those days. Unfortunately, the replaced valve was faulty. Jonathan had yet another heart attack at sixteen, leading to replacement of the valve a second time.

Following two open-heart surgeries and two valve replacements, he was now on a transplant list with an imminent need to replace his failing heart. He took several potent medicines, including one that thinned his blood.

Because the second valve was plastic, whenever his heartbeat, you could hear him tick, tick, tick…like a grandfather clock. To his family, it was an endearing sound, and of course gave new meaning to the word "ticker". It also revealed his emotions because whenever he was nervous, angry, or tired, his heart began to beat faster and the noise grew even more pronounced.

Due to his illness, he struggled to find his place in life. Oftentimes, he was too weak to excel at the sports he had once enjoyed and, with no real identity among the athletes he knew, felt he no longer "fit in" anywhere.

Though Jonathan was on the donor list, most of us knew getting a heart would be a long shot. Complicating matters, the Jarvis, the pioneer version of an artificial heart, still had a long way to go before it was widely available.

Nonetheless, that last summer we spent together was amazing. As my first "team partner", Jonathan taught me firsthand that each day is a gift. With him, I was given a rare glimpse, at sixteen, into understanding how precious and fragile life is (while my teenage friends were running around, convinced they were invincible).

Jonathan and I talked about everything that summer. We went to many places, met many people, and used each minute as though it were our last. He wanted to model for a living—and was handsome enough to pull it off, though some considered him "cocky" and "a know-it-all". Among his other goals: drive a Porsche, do "great" things, and enjoy life to the fullest.

His attitude was contagious. As the result of an insurance settlement, he was awarded a large sum of money. Now he could really make things happen. The first thing he decided to do was launch his modeling career and hire an agent.

He wasn't able to buy a Porsche, so he settled for a blue, convertible Karmann Ghia. Still, to me he was being brave. I think he knew even then that his life would be shorter than he had hoped, and that he needed to take advantage of each day that remained. While his brave was big, so was the fear that drove him. But he never let that fear stop him from living.

We often hear people who face dying say they live each day as though it's their last. Jonathan did just that. At the end of that summer, we parted as better people, who were richer in experiences.

Eighteen months passed. I went to college and hadn't spoken with Jonathan in quite a while. Life had gotten busy. Letters were few and far between, and although I had intended to reach out, I didn't. I would come to regret not doing so.

In December of my senior year of college, I received word that Jonathan had passed away. He was in the process of moving in with his fiancé. While shifting boxes in their new home, he lay down to rest and never woke up.

While it was a relief to know that he was at a place in his life where he was happy, and had found love, I was also deeply saddened.

He was buried near his grandfather in Clovis, New Mexico, where his mother grew up. I went later that summer to visit his gravesite and spend some time reflecting on the many things his friendship had brought to me. His legacy gave me a rare glimpse into the power of raw and oftentimes unguarded fear—how to really open up and share what scares you most.

Jonathan taught me that talking about your fears made them less scary. I took that lesson into my future relationships, vowing I would never be afraid to share my innermost fears. It also gave me greater depth in many of the friendships I experienced after Jonathan.

He had learned to dream big and live brave, never knowing how long life would allow him to stay. He loved big, too, convincing me that everyone matters in life. I realized that as in a relay race when a baton is passed from one to the next, our friends and loved ones also carry us to the next place.

Through Jonathan, I learned to take chances and at least made an attempt to do what I dreamed. He modeled for a short time, but after completing his first runway show, realized his health was too poor to keep up with the demands of the career. Yet, that one experience helped him taste success.

His brave was big, and he showed me a little glimpse into just how big brave can be when you know you have nothing to lose. I still wonder if Jonathan died knowing he had done much of what he wanted to do, or what gifts he had left behind for others.

The first of my team builders, Jonathan was my role model and my inspiration, though he probably never knew the part he had played in getting me where I am today. As a result of his influence, I promised myself I wouldn't die without doing as much of what I had set out to do as possible. This was the power of his legacy.

***

Colleen Jones, my father's childhood friend, was another person who had a major impact on my life. My father grew up the son of an alcoholic and needed a place of refuge. It was Colleen's mother who took him in, making him feel like part of their family.

After she married, Colleen moved to Florida where her husband, Charles, opened an automotive shop. As an adult, my father reconnected with Colleen and decided that we were close enough to visit. When we arrived, I noted the house was a sprawling brick ranch, beautifully decorated— even somewhat "fancy" in my opinion.

We were shown where to sleep, passing doors that sectioned off what appeared to be a sunken living room. That left me curious. I asked where the doors led, and Colleen said it was their personal home gym.

As we opened the entrance to this wondrous chamber, the bright lights, mirrors, and steel machines made me feel like I had just stepped onto a movie set. My eyes were drawn to the machines while I scanned the room. I checked out the large chain cables, the blue cushion seats, and all the stations that beckoned to every body part. I thought it had the look of a medieval torture chamber—only much more inviting.

This place is amazing, I thought, and I wanted to know more about what these machines actually did. That's where my fascination with gyms began, along with the idea that it might be something I wanted to make an important part of my life.

Colleen and Charles were a beautiful couple who clearly loved and respected each other.

Even when they worked out together, they held hands and shared laughs.

Every evening before bed, they went to their home gym and worked out for an hour or more, emerging transformed, glowing, and happy. When I witnessed this, it was electric.

I wanted to be like them. Their lifestyle fit them well, and they seemed so in love.

A glow of health and smiles made me want to know more about them and what they shared. It was then and there that I made the connection that a healthy life and a healthy love went together. The power of that perception would be with me for the rest of my life.

At the tender age of twelve, I wanted to know more about those two facets of life and began believing that combination, healthy and happy, was a recipe for success, especially since I had experienced the opposite in our home.

My father's military mentality meant he took a tough stance against what he deemed as "undisciplined". When he gave my mother a hard time, it was mostly about her size.

'Are you going to eat that?' He'd say, reminding her that she needed to lose weight.

When they first met and then married, she was a trim one hundred twenty pounds. But over the span of several years, her weight ballooned to more than two hundred, where she remained for the rest of her life.

I watched the toll on her self-esteem and how she slowly began to withdraw. In time, when I married, I ironically found myself in a similar situation.

Though I chose a man who was fit and in incredible shape, and though he was willing to workout with me to stay healthy, he held the same qualities of my father—casually reminding me that I was "too heavy" or hinting that I needed to lose weight.

I now realize I used his attitude to blame him and create issues that weren't actually his.

The love I needed had to come from myself, and a faith in myself that I deserved the love I was looking for. Yet my body became the roadblock for the full scope of love I knew deep down I deserved.

I believe today that negative mental conditioning and my beliefs from growing up and seeing this struggle in my family are what eventually led me to natural bodybuilding. Through this newfound competitive sport, I was able to chip away at my self-doubt, inspired by the lifestyle of Colleen and Charles.

After several years of competing and doing quite well, I found the need to reach out and find them in order to tell them how much their influence meant to me, and to thank them for being positive role models. Facebook helped me find Charles and reconnect. I sent him a message. He and Colleen were now part of my "team", I told him.

The following year, with my parents joining us, we returned to Florida to have Thanksgiving together and celebrate like old times. After dinner, Charles worked out with me, encouraging me as we reignited a great friendship and mentorship. It was a special time, and one for which I remained grateful long after we had departed.

At sixty-four, Charles still had the best and biggest biceps I had ever seen. However, his heart was the biggest, most powerful muscle he possessed, due to his kindness and generosity. On 2 July 2013, as he was walking to his mailbox, he collapsed and died.

When I heard the news, I could not stop crying. I felt so fortunate to have had a chance to reconnect and say all that I had wanted to say.

He had made a difference in my life and he knew it. He had always used those six powerful words with me: 'I am so proud of you.' I am also a better person today because he chose to make me a small part of his family.

***

Alice Montgomery was a lovely woman with a Southern drawl and blonde hair the color of sunshine. Although she was heavyset, what you noticed first about her was the bright light that followed her into the room. Her laugh was contagious and her charm irresistible. Alice was from a small town in Western North Carolina and much of her family still lives there today.

Being from Alabama, where your heart, not your zip code, is what makes you "southern", Ms. Alice kept me grounded by reminding me we should measure our success by how many people we attempt to connect with, and how many connect with us.

Shortly after moving to a home on a cul-de-sac in North Carolina, I was standing at my mailbox when Ms. Alice walked up and invited me to a Bible study. My husband was working as a consultant, traveling Monday through Friday, so it was just my three-year-old daughter and me during the week.

New to the area, I was teaching a few aerobics classes in local gyms, but other than that I knew only a few people and did not get out much. Ms. Alice's invitation to the Bible study began a lifelong friendship that would become part of the team-building that helped form me.

She had three children, two out of college and one still in high school. Mr. Buck, her husband, was a hard-working construction manager and foreman for a large construction firm in the area. He was a salt-of-the-earth type who rounded out this "perfect" little family.

Of course, I knew there was no such thing as a perfect family, and they would have agreed that they weren't the perfect family! But to watch them and be around them, you would have a hard time convincing me otherwise. They were as close to "perfect" as I had ever witnessed.

With my husband constantly on the road, my daughter and I found ourselves at Ms. Alice's up to five nights a week. She had us over for dinner on weeknights, gave her a bath (warming her towel in the dryer), read her a bedtime story, and sent us home with leftovers for the next day.

Alice's involvement in our lives gave me confidence along with extra hours in the day because her family took such good care of my daughter, allowing me time to begin a more serious journey toward my fitness and work goals.

Ms. Alice always encouraged me, asking me when I would be on TV, buying sessions from me that she would never use, and asking me questions for advice that she would never take. She made me feel like the smartest trainer on Earth, even if she did like her wine and good Southern comfort food a bit too much. Through her love and generous support, she made me believe that I was capable of achieving most anything.

For his part, Mr. Buck searched for my dog when she wandered away, fixed anything I couldn't fix myself when my husband was on the road, and when I was pregnant with my second child, stashed chocolate bars for me whenever I needed a fix.

When my son was born, it was Ms. Alice who was in the delivery room. Even today, my kids know no greater love (outside of our own family) than that of Ms. Alice and Mr. Buck. She still cheers for me after all these years, though we're more than three hundred miles apart.

I can't fully describe how much I love Alice and her family and what a difference they made in my life. It's something special when people love you that much, but even more special when they love your children as well. They form the cornerstones of my team.

***

Sometimes, building your team requires starting over.

Kiki and Neninee (my nicknames for them) became my first two friends shortly after moving to Asheville. There was an event called "an adventure race", a fifty-mile competition that combined trail running, mountain biking, and kayaking; all three to be completed in twelve hours or less.

My husband was also invited to join, and following the event there was a get-together at a local pizza joint. It was there I met Kiki, a single woman with beautiful green eyes, long strawberry-blond hair, and a giant smile. She was an admissions counselor at a local liberal arts college.

Kiki and I couldn't be more different in our social or political outlook. She was a peace-loving Democrat who believed in things I didn't even understand. A conservationist, activist, and any other "ist" you could think of, Kiki cared about everything. But people were her specialty.

I also met Neninee, who is tall with long, gazelle-like legs, dark brown hair and brown eyes, topped by a sweet voice. A first-grade teacher, it was obvious she had a kind heart and a way with children, asking us in her nurturing way if we needed drinks or a napkin. Neninee's husband was on one of the teams and along with him, she enjoyed running and being active.

Neninee, Kiki, and I found we shared a common interest in all things ambitious. We became an instant running family and our motto was *Love your guts*—that stuff inside you that makes you work hard and never give up.

We took annual ski vacations together for years, competed in countless marathons, half marathons, two fifty-mile adventure races, and a number of smaller races. We lived through highs and lows in our personal lives, supporting each other through various hardships. Besides running, we spent time together celebrating birthdays, having cookouts, and most of all, building goals and dreams.

Kiki and Neninee attended any event I'd ask them to, even if they didn't know what it was or why I was participating. They made Asheville, with its newly acquired "New Age" vibe, work better for me, and eventually helped me begin to call it home. In the process, they convinced me that I could do anything. They are still two of my closest friends.

In Miranda Lambert's song *The House That Built Me*, she says, "You leave home and you move on and you do the best you can. I got lost in this whole world and forgot who

I am." But Kiki and Neninee are the part of my team meant to remind me who I am—even if I don't always agree.

***

Some members join your team simply to boot you along, nudging you with steel-toed boots, rather than with warm fuzzy slippers. These are the people in our lives with little gift for mercy and zero bedside manner.

They are the antithesis of encouragement and can be the source of both pain and grief. Yet, they can also be an important part of your team because they force you to succeed through proving—to them and to yourself—that you can do it.

Mac had a gym not far from my home, full of Nautilus equipment and big egos, mostly his. Well-known by people in the profession as "the man" in natural bodybuilding in our area—and I would argue perhaps throughout the South—he was considered the best.

When I made the decision to compete, I also decided it was time to hire him. If you wanted to do well, I was advised, he was the go-to guy.

Mac soon shared that he had once slept on the couch of Arthur Jones, designer and creator of Nautilus gym equipment, and that he, Mac, helped deliver the equipment whenever it was ready for its new home.

Arthur Jones was no doubt a genius. But from what I understood, he was also a jerk, and Mac exhibited some of those same traits. Mac tended not to speak to you; he spoke at you. He also expected his clients to learn from his lectures, as he didn't have time to mess around. If you didn't

114

learn from what he told you, you needed to find another trainer.

At our first meeting, I laid out my plan. I told him I was thirty-nine, had two children, and a body that needed a transformation through natural bodybuilding. As I stated my plan, I remembered how ridiculous I felt, and by the look on Mac's face, he was about to confirm my worst fears.

'Just because you pay money and show up, that's no guarantee of success,' he said bluntly. 'But *possibly* with hard work and a clean diet, you might make it.'

I agreed to his terms, and although I was filled with more fear than excitement, I signed up with plans to compete a few months later.

Coming up was a drug-free/drug-tested natural bodybuilding competition in South Carolina. Drug-free and drug-tested did not mean people who used steroids didn't show up, but it was a way to keep them from actually competing. Nevertheless, this natural contest was one of the best places for new people starting out. As I filled out the forms, I promised myself that if I started this, I would finish it.

I worked out three days a week and did the same routine almost every workout. I couldn't listen to music, and if Mac had his way, I wouldn't be allowed to talk either. Nonetheless, I found myself nervously chatting at almost every session.

Mac was not amused. A tall, white-haired man, he wore wide circular glasses over prominent eyes. With his white mustache and thick physique, whenever he donned a red, tight hammer strength Lycra shirt, it made his muscles even more prominent. Feisty and stubborn, he worked hard. He ran clients through his gym for up to twelve hours a day, six days a week, taking an hour most days for his own workout.

I felt a little like the Karate Kid during our workouts as he barked out his orders. Anytime I would ask a question, he whipped his head around and fixed his stare on me. 'If you want to be a bodybuilder,' he'd say, 'you have to lift the heavy weights.'

Sometimes, when I came to weigh in, he told me I'd make a great bodybuilder if we could just get the fat off.

Though I'll never know for sure, my perception was that Mac didn't much like me. Yet that really wasn't what mattered. I was there to reach my goals.

I learned a valuable lesson along the way: *Don't get distracted just because people don't like you.* I also learned later that Mac kept a small sign near his desk that read: *I Hate Everyone.*

Make a Note of It.

I introduced him to a friend in phenomenal shape who had had a successful career competing. She said she was looking for a new trainer and was interested in working with him. She soon became his favorite client and he would tell me that if I wanted to make it, I would need to be more like her.

I remember telling myself this wasn't all I had in my life, and that I didn't have to give up my life for this sport in order to be successful. I also knew in my heart that just stepping on stage and looking like I belonged would be a great goal to reach.

Would grumpy Mac ever realize and appreciate that as well? Or did that even matter? It made knowing what your purpose and plan were even more critical. When you have a plan and know what to do, fueled by purpose, you are less likely to get lost in perception.

Being brave here meant giving Mac permission to think what he wanted to about my motivations, and knowing his thoughts didn't make or break me.

Despite the fact that he had worked with some of the best names in bodybuilding (competitors like Arnold Schwarzenegger and other Mr. Universe winners), had competed in several competitions, won countless trophies, and authored a book, he still seemed to me not a content or happy person. I wondered if all those years of evaluating people, and of course managing your own ego and issues, could leave one jaded.

However, he was smart and great at what he did. What he taught me as part of my team is that sometimes hard work isn't the only thing you need to win. You also need guts and a healthy amount of fear in order to keep going.

Whenever I wanted to quit, or not work as hard, Mac was quick to remind me that my competition was just down the street working harder than I was. If I quit, she wins, he said.

He was right, which in turn forced me to push myself.

Now, years later, even though he was my most reluctant "team member", I thank him every day for adding another—though sometimes painful—building block toward making me the person I have become.

In reality, there will be people on your team who will both push and pull you. They can help guide you toward what you want in life and might even show you the way, or they can get behind you and shove you forward. Either way, they are there to help you on your journey, if you don't allow them to alter your self-image.

"There is no enemy outside if there's no enemy within," was one of Mac's favorite quotes. He was right about that, too.

Sometimes they help us find the enemy within us. These are the inner battles we carry around with us, and end up waging against ourselves. Some might call them "demons". I prefer to perceive them as "the circus in my head".

And I'm the ringleader, with a brave that gets bigger each day.

Chapter Eight
The Circus in My Head

It's been a long road learning about the things that can make or break me. In the journey to find greater success, I have discovered that each level of experience has created a greater level of understanding.

Over the years, I've been fascinated by the mind-body connection and have studied extensively the way the body and brain interact (or don't). I've read numerous medical journals and books about the brain and its function in an effort to better understand my clients and why some are more successful than others.

I hoped to find a magic key or smoking gun pointing to what people say to themselves that causes some to succeed with leaps and bounds while others crash and burn right out of the gate.

The incongruence of the words and actions of not only my clients, but my friends and even myself has been enlightening to say the least. I would eat healthy every day, but didn't count the calories if I went through a drive-through or when no one was looking.

I would exercise and feel as though I was killing myself, but more often than not stop just shy of one hundred percent. Or I'd quit with the capacity to do more work remaining. I would have a late supper on Sunday nights with the best of intentions for Monday morning and find myself making excuses for Taco Tuesday and of course—don't forget the margarita.

I would stop and start over more times than I could count. I had excuses and reasons that few people could create as well as I did. I crafted great stories and made up just enough reality to believe them.

Yet the same person, me, could do two full Ironman races, two half-Ironman races, countless 5k and 10k runs, four marathons, two 50-mile adventure races, plus body build for five years and weigh a hundred twenty-six pounds at age thirty-nine, taking home ten trophies while competing.

I was even an anomaly to myself. How could I be two people? Or was the story I was telling myself the true difference? The Bible tells us that words have the power of life and death (Proverbs 18:21)—a profound statement from an insightful place.

In her work, English author and speaker Marisa Peer, who created Rapid Transformational Technique has been helping people get unstuck for years. She says that our words create our actions and that by changing our words, we can change our actions.

But it's really changing our beliefs. Changing our beliefs takes longer, so changing the way we talk to ourselves, the words we use to describe ourselves or our actions, can be the catalyst to changing everything.

In her early days, Peer worked with Jane Fonda and taught aerobics in her L.A. studio for a number of years. She was able to observe the behavior of several of the women in the class who struggled with eating disorders and recognized the disease was rooted in the same belief of not being enough.

When Peer talked with participants and dug deeper, she found that everyone seemed to end up in the same place with the fear that they weren't enough: weren't skinny enough, weren't smart enough, weren't pretty enough, which was underscored by a Hollywood culture that rewarded only those who were thin, intelligent, and beautiful.

Today, the age of technology and social media keeps a constant watch on what is enough or who is good enough, and like it or not, we find ourselves competing with the same old cultural beliefs.

How do we learn to counter that? I came from a place where, when someone said something negative, you used it to power yourself to the next level. What I wasn't aware of was that I would have competing beliefs within myself. I would use what someone said about me that was negative to fuel my behavior to respond positively, but ended up using twice as much energy to offset self-doubt.

For example, I was told in high school that we didn't have a girls' soccer team and I couldn't play with the boys for two reasons: 1) I wasn't a boy and 2) Girls weren't as good at soccer as boys.

I knew that if I could keep up, I might even excel. Undeterred, I asked if I could be the exception. I tried out for the team. Despite the merciless hazing that followed, I was soon accepted through my sheer tenacity and grit, showing up every day.

After two years of playing, I worked my way onto the team and into the hearts of my fellow players. I remember the year that we won the championships and everyone got trophies.

The coach made sure my trophy was in the shape of a girl.

'Your trophy has boobs,' my teammates joked. But it didn't matter. I knew I had to constantly outwork the guys in order to be taken seriously. I couldn't be "weak", and I had to be "the best".

What I *should* have told myself was, "You are brave enough to try out for the boys' team and that's enough."

This pattern of both negative and positive feedback became exhausting over time. I just didn't realize it until much later in life.

If anyone had to spend even a minute in my head, I'm certain they would not only think I was crazy, but they would also wonder what type of war I was waging on myself. I call this craziness the "circus in my head".

The elephants in my circus are my body image; the monkeys are my thoughts; the lions are how I treat myself. I bring out the clowns when I know I'm being too hard on myself and need some levity.

The elephants are on display most often, and the ones I deal with most.

Even at my lightest weight, I believed I could do better and that I was still too "big". My thighs rubbed together no matter what my size, my hips were too big, and my butt worthy of the song, *Baby Got Back.*

As I age and begin to care less about those things, I wish someone had helped me see then how important it is to be kind to myself instead of the constant beatings I administered to myself.

Now, when I hear clients disparage themselves, I always ask, 'Would you treat your best friend the way you treat yourself?' The answer is almost always, 'No way.'

I still struggle with this dilemma, not knowing how to appreciate my good qualities and nurture them. It's much easier to create an all-out assault on myself and all my flaws, making it hard to love and accept myself as a whole person.

Don't you think most people find that to be true?

Marianne Williamson, an American spiritual teacher, reminds us, "Often, our deepest fear is not that we are inadequate. Our deepest fear is that we are powerful beyond measure. It is our light, not our darkness that most frightens us."

I see this often in my life and in the lives of my clients. Our circus is a sweeping assault on our bodies that begins in our head and ends when we grow scared enough to stop striving for perfection.

Our elephants remind us that being a healthy weight just isn't in our DNA. Our monkeys tell us we are not good enough, or will never be "strong" enough.

I travel with this circus just as I would a real ringside event, moving from one situation to another, setting up the tent, and handing out popcorn as others witness me managing the show. However, it has also helped me realize the power of the mind, which controls nearly everything, and for that insightful gift, I am grateful.

At the same time, I recognize that I need a sanctuary, not a circus. I need a nurturing environment, not a party that can turn bad at any minute. I need to clean house in my head and start over again. I need to end the "circus cycle" or it will become a *vicious* cycle instead.

While each of us needs inspiration as a means to do well, we tend to use shame to help us move forward. Shaming can get results, but they are short-term because you can't stay in an uncomfortable place for long.

Shame tells you to lose weight. Comfort tells you to work toward becoming your best self. In the middle lane is your true, authentic self—a person constantly striving to become the best he or she can be without the emotional beating that comes with punishing themselves through shame.

I remember encountering a friend following a dramatic weight loss and asking him what helped him most to lose the weight. He said his trigger was that he needed gallbladder surgery and the surgeon had referred to him as "morbidly obese".

When he heard the surgeon describe him in those terms, he was so embarrassed he genuinely *wanted* to lose the weight. Shame can get you there, but he has since realized that staying there requires that you learn to like the whole person that you are. Ironically, this story is of the goalie from that same soccer team I had played on. We were having lunch twenty years later as he told me this story.

What if I changed the conversation in my head and created a sanctuary instead of a circus? That would mean formulating a plan and creating steps to overcome all the work I had put into being unkind to myself.

My first step: seek advice through friends, music, and books. I found refuge in Donald Miller's statement that is paraphrased in the book, *Blue Like Jazz,* "Don't end where you begin".

This phrase is found in the bible in Zechariah 4:10 with a little different twist. "Do not despise these small beginnings"—keep pressing for the good.

Training for the Ironman taught me a lot about my belief systems. What I focused on most was my primary goal. Yet, at the time, staying focused was not easy. I was going through a separation and had to move three times in three months.

That made my entire event training all the more difficult. I managed to get things done, but I fell below the minimum of what I normally was able to accomplish.

To offset my inability to train the way I wanted and needed to, I would instead watch YouTube videos about Ironman competitions, visualizing it was me working hard in the training room and not a random competitor.

The benefits of visualization gained support decades ago in a university study that showed a combined physical practice/mental practice regimen was almost as good as physical practice alone. Free-throw shooters who shot a hundred free throws a day improved twenty-two percent by the end of the study, while those who shot fifty, and visualized fifty, improved by twenty-one percent.

Following that example, I visualized myself crossing the finish line of the Ironman competition, and the tasks I had to undertake in order to complete it. I didn't break any records, but I did cross that line, and I learned a little more about the power of mind and changing my internal messages.

I saw the finish line in my head almost every minute of every day leading up to the thrilling moment that I crossed the line on 7 November 2015.

In my head, I finally found my brave and became the ringleader of my circus.

Changing the circus to a sanctuary also means you have to bury old beliefs and cultivate new ones. I wish I had a dollar for every time I was asked how someone could lose five or ten pounds quickly. My standard response: *Get serious*. That might not have been the best response, but consider the question.

If you want something to happen fast, you're likely to react with an emotional response. But if you're committed to a greater outcome, you understand there is no quick fix and therefore hard work and oftentimes teamwork is involved. Would you go to a college admissions counselor and ask how to get a four-year degree in a month?

Or attend a culinary arts school and ask them to teach you one fabulous meal and then award you chef credentials? Of course not.

In my presentations, I tell people don't worry about what you can't do. Concentrate on what you *can* do. What are your best traits? What can you change? What will change you?

Clients ask if I can make up diets or meal plans for them, but I've found it's much better if the client comes up with the basics and I help them modify what needs changing.

These are people who tend to feel they can't be trusted or left alone to make their own decisions. They want the guardrails in place. They want fences built around their circus to keep the animals at bay. We've all been "those people" at times.

I also believe that you must be able to do well without the fear of a mean, nasty trainer (which, by the way, most of us are not) telling you what to do. The truth is, we are connecting who you are with who you want to be, and helping to teach you how to bridge the gap between the two.

Let's stick with the circus analogy for now.

Imagine a lion tamer with his whip as he cracks it near a snarling, swatting beast. In reality, this whip serves no real purpose because the lion could easily rise up, attack the tamer, and eat him. As trainers, we want to refrain from all-out attacks, while still keeping the lion at bay.

Why? Because number one, this whip-cracking approach usually doesn't work. And two, as mentioned earlier, anything that is shame-based is generally counter-productive. For example, flogging is a form of self-punishment found mostly in Arab countries when Muslims take their sacred journey to Mecca.

Leather straps are attached to a handle to form a whip, which the person holds en route. Along the way, they beat themselves on the back and body to symbolize their disdain for themselves, their physical body, and their desire to be better by beating away the "bad". But is it effective? Not for long.

In truth, people do this to themselves each day, but instead of using a whip, they use words. They may be doing really well and then all of a sudden, they make a wrong turn. Out comes the whip and the flogging begins.

It's far better to run away from the circus and find a sanctuary. But how do you make the change? I begin with ten mindful minutes every morning.

In a 2015 TED Talk, mindfulness expert Andy Puddicombe, a former Buddhist monk with a degree in circus arts, maintains that ten minutes each day can change your entire life. Since I suffer from a severe form of attention-deficit disorder (ADD), I can tell you from experience that the first ten "mindful" minutes are like chasing a ball of thought through a musical sing-a-long.

Over time, I added soft music to soothe my brain and practiced daily almost before my feet hit the floor.

I review my intentions daily, say positive things to myself, and make a commitment to treat myself well during the day. I spend time visualizing how good my workouts will be, the food I will eat, and how it will feel to be successful. Other times I count off the minutes during my stretching, which has helped tremendously. This is where creating a sanctuary and quieting the circus begins for me.

***

Behind the scenes, there is practice, practice, practice, and other things the "audience" never sees. The goal is to host the best show possible while weeding out what works and what doesn't.

As a society, we are inundated with potions, lotions, and all things chemical. For more than twenty years, I have tried many diet products, mostly because I'm like everyone else and want to figure out what works. Some left me with shaky hands or too nauseous to eat. Some resulted in talking a hundred miles an hour because I was amped.

Some just left me wondering if Solomon in Ecclesiastes 1:9 was right when he said, "There is nothing new under the sun."

From the early 1800s, when snake oil sales representatives came to town with their products and promises, positive results were rare. Today, many of the products on the market for weight loss have more affect as a placebo than they do for achieving real results.

I am certain if there actually was a product that could create quick, painless weight loss, we would all know about it. Instead, we chase the "miracles" of weight-loss products, while the weight-loss industry hits the trillion-dollar mark in revenue for its mostly worthless merchandise.

At the same time, obesity rates continue to climb. The U.S. is at an all-time high for obesity rates and ensuing medical complications. We don't want to hear it, but hard work and discipline are the antidotes. I have witnessed this principle many times in my training and in working with my clients.

Sorry, folks—no magic bullets and no shortcuts.

When eating within my allotted food guidelines and caloric levels, I lose weight. When eating too much, an amount greater than my guidelines, I gain. During the thirty-six weeks of training for a bodybuilding competition, I worked out three days a week, one hour a day, minus cardio.

When I stepped on the stage at a hundred twenty-six pounds, the lowest weight I've been since tenth grade, I did so with no potions, no pills, and no snake oil. Learning that hard work is the only element needed for success changed how I worked on myself in my head.

Furthermore, the right attitude—leaving the circus behind—along with the right team and support, can make you unstoppable.

I also realized that if I didn't sell tickets to the circus in my head, no one would come to see the show. I gained freedom by retiring the elephant, shipping the wild animals elsewhere, and refusing to perform in a three-ring circus.

However, just like Barnum and Bailey, I wanted to leave a legacy behind. What would it take to achieve that? Hard work was the only answer I found.

How can you create your own legacy? Start by thinking about what or who is the most important thing in your life. For me, it is my children. I want to leave them an example of healthy living and serve as their role model in the meantime.

From a national perspective, childhood obesity is on the rise, with unhealthy kids facing the many grown-up problems that arise from poor diet, nutrition, and lack of exercise. Diabetes in children is increasing, too, along with heart disease and hypertension. According to the Centers for Disease Control (CDC), our children could be the first generation in which they might not outlive their parents. That's a frightening thought.

In my own hometown, I've seen the battle rage between childhood obesity and chronic illness. It's difficult to put blame on one person and one cause. But I believe that you live what you see, and you practice what you know.

Whenever I talk to clients about their eating and health habits, invariably a story is shared about how they have grown up eating certain things (mostly bad) and avoiding certain healthy habits (like exercise). These patterns or habits continue to be part of their issues as they become adults because their behaviors stem from repetition.

In my own case, my mom was a fantastic cook and my dad could concoct a mean gravy. Most dinners at my house were standard meat and potatoes. Monday night was beans and cornbread.

To this day, if you show up at my parents' house on Monday night, there is a significant chance you'll be eating beans and cornbread. My mother also insisted that we try her desserts once we finished everything on our plate, and so we did.

As I began my wellness journey, this pattern of overeating (and eating the wrong food) would be one of the lions I constantly needed to tame. How I was raised had a direct effect on my eating habits. While I vowed not to pass these issues on to my children that was much easier said than done.

As parents, we all know our kids are prey to influences outside our control. I have found myself at odds with school lunches, societal pressure, and the reality that junk food is cheap and convenient. I also realized that I would need to be a leader in my home regarding food in order to make a difference in my children's lives. It would take a delicate balance to help them navigate these tricky waters.

My daughter, for example, is tall and leggy and was a healthy eater most of her life. For several years, she made shakes for breakfast and designed her own lunches to take to school. We never had soda in our home, and she kept a water bottle with her at all times.

In her high school years, she fell prey to unhealthy food, while developing a sweet tooth.

However, now as an independent woman living in New York City, she meal preps, goes to the gym three days a week, and is quick to connect how her week is going based on how well she has taken care of herself.

It's my goal to continue to ensure that the choices we make in our home are healthy ones. I never pushed her to make my choices, but her own. I've seen too many mothers push their daughters so much that they end up being plagued by weight issues.

Mothers who are obese, yet who want me to help their daughters maintain a normal weight, have hired me as a trainer and I have to wonder, *how do you expect your child to eat healthy when you don't?*

Sometimes I find it is the "skinny family" with a single child who eats too much, and sometimes it's a situation in which everyone in the family is obese and that is the "norm". These are tough environments to overcome. In those cases, I have learned to say thank you, but no thank you to mothers with family members who are not totally in the effort together.

Remember my client Nick from chapter one whose entire family was overweight? Nick and I worked together successfully until it was time for his mother to step in. However, she didn't want to take over the responsibility of helping keep her son on track. Nor did she want to be a role model, despite the fact she didn't like being heavy herself.

Not long after Nick began to show success in his weight-loss program, his progress began to decline. Eventually, it disappeared. As with any goal in which you are struggling with addiction issues, whether food, drugs, or other substances, it's imperative to have a strong support system around you. Without it, success is hard to achieve and maintain.

My son has the same attention-deficit disorder that I struggle with, and like me, his behavior is greatly affected by food. I can tell when he's had too much sugar and not enough protein solely by how he behaves. I discovered his food-based behavior early on because of an asthma condition present at birth.

After a two-day stay in the hospital, he was taking breathing treatments that left him jittery and anxious. It was critical that he become strong and healthy.

Following my own research, I learned that lean protein (like chicken and turkey), a heart-healthy protein, might prevent his system from overreacting. My son also experienced greater problems with his asthma if he consumed too many dairy products.

At his preschool, a state auditor told my son's teacher he *must* drink milk because it was a state mandate, and that even though I had researched the topic and had a doctor's order, we couldn't be exempt. The teacher explained that my alternative was soy milk, even though the research indicated soy milk wasn't any better.

The preschool auditor was Chinese and her family was from mainland China. When I asked if the kids in her country drank milk, she responded, 'No.' Then added, 'But this isn't China.'

The circus in my head was now back in full swing. I was soon waging an all-out war with a dietitian on Facebook about this same topic. She was someone I knew who represented a large chain of grocery stores in the area. The incident began when one of my friends, also on Facebook, asked me if she needed to drink milk.

She said she felt that milk was making her and her children sick (problems with gas and bloating), which are characteristics of being lactose intolerant.

She was concerned about giving up milk because she thought her children needed vitamin D. I explained to her that research supports other ways to get Vitamin D besides from milk, and that if she wanted to discontinue it at least that was a way to find out if they were allergic.

The dietician promptly butted in, saying I had no business telling this mother to stop drinking milk as she, the dietician, "knew" it was good for everyone. But because she wasn't in very good shape herself, I questioned her authority and opinions, much to her displeasure.

If you think that's a harsh judgment, look around. Healthcare providers are some of the worst offenders in terms of their own weight issues, yet we rely on them to lead us to good health and wellness.

Not questioning those in authority is another reason the circus in our heads rises to the surface. Taking everything at face value is why we fail at what we know is the right thing to do. That's also why we need a sanctuary to keep us from going off the rails when it comes to our own personal health and the health of our families.

So, how do we bridge this disconnect between the head and heart when the two so often don't match?

Start by listening to yourself and stop believing everything you read and hear. Use critical skills to question, question, and question before you make a final decision that can affect you for the rest of your life. Do your research, check your sources and don't assume "the experts" know more than you do.

Then ask yourself: Are you caring toward others, but careless when it comes to yourself? Do you pretend to be "good" with your nutrition and fitness when your body aches from the excess weight you carry around? Do you fail to get enough sleep, causing you to stay unfocused, tired, and cranky? Fix the mind, where your sanctuary should reside, and the head and body will follow.

And leave your circus in the dust where it belongs.

Victory will come when you admit your stress level is high and you feed yourself the best food possible. Then remember that when you need nursing and care most, that's the worst time to bring back the circus.

Creating a sanctuary means that the circus noise in your head must be replaced with something that can help move you forward. The negative boos from the crowd in my head can sometimes be overwhelming, so I create a sound that helps me move in the right direction.

YouTube has been a great place for me to find this type of positive feedback and insight. I use motivational videos and often listen to them over and over to rebuild what I know my head can quickly erase.

Eric Thomas is someone I can recite in my sleep and, more often than not, I imagine that he is talking directly to me. Thomas, an author, motivational speaker, and pastor, is well known to his fans as the "Hip-Hop Preacher".

He tells the story of a man who wants to be rich. The man's guru instructs him to come to the beach. There, the guru brings his disciple into the water where he holds him under until the man must either fight to take a breath or drown.

"When you want something as bad as you want to breathe, then you'll be successful," the guru tells the young man.

I wanted to meet Eric Thomas. I love his energy, passion, and swagger. I find him compelling enough to make me believe I can have it all, too. His approach is straight up, as though he is talking directly with you. I wanted to see him face-to-face and thank him for being who he is.

One day, while at the Detroit airport with friends on my way to Asheville, I spotted him talking on the phone. Eric Thomas was right in front of me! Undaunted, I walked up and spoke to him from my heart, with no preconceived notion of how he would respond.

'Holy cow, it's so great to see you,' I sputtered.

Though I embarrassed myself, he promptly hung up the phone, telling his friend, 'I'll call you back, man,' with his eyes and attention fixed on me.

I told him how much I appreciated the motivational gifts he shared and how awesome he was, as well as the significant impact he had made on my life. I realized this was a rare chance I have been given, so I hugged him, got a photo with him, and thanked him for being kind enough to say hello.

When I returned to my gate to join my friends, they asked how I knew Eric, assuming our meeting was personal. They had seen us hugging and talking together.

'He's someone who is kind of a hero of mine,' I responded.

In that moment, I felt things shift for me, as though by divine appointment. I promised myself this moment would be a turning point—a time when I would conquer my fear and finally, truly believe my future was bright, even if the circus returned to town.

When the fear kicked in and the circus did return—as it invariably will—I vowed to release the monkeys, calm the lions, and make the elephants grab the tail in front of them, following each other out.

All along, I realized they had been waiting for my cue. I was the ringleader, and I had the power to either make them perform or lead them to a sanctuary where, along with me, they could flourish.

You have the same choice. You can choose to welcome the circus back to town or you can send it away, spending your time and energy on creating your own success.

Is your brave big enough to accomplish such a feat? If the answer is yes, be sure you know two things: What does success mean to you, and how exactly do you measure it?

Chapter Nine
Power Over
Poisonous Perceptions

Have you ever wondered how big your brave really is? I know we practice brave when we wear that shirt we bought despite it being outside our comfort zone in style or color. We practice brave when we make our concerns or hopes known for the first time to someone we love, or when we experience a difficult relationship.

But what do we know about the boundaries of our brave? How wide is it? How vast?

How deep does our brave run? How do we even begin to figure that out?

I once again credit being a military brat and that lifestyle to having a healthy dose of brave. I wasn't as afraid of rejection as I was of isolation, so I approached people who could potentially be friends despite the risk of rejection.

I was and have always been curious about people and the world, and so I would bravely ask questions or step into discomfort to figure out what makes people and places who and what they are.

I have experienced some awesome things in my life that some say require bravery. I have run with the bulls in Pamplona, jumped out of an airplane twice, skied some pretty crazy places, and moved to Korea at twenty-two with no family or friends there to help me figure out the landscape.

I was hired as an independent contractor by one of the largest companies in my area to teach and train in workplace wellness. I told my husband of twenty-one years I wanted a divorce. From time to time, I have been known to say things and do things that many would consider brave.

But how do you get the courage to move from one checker square to the other? How do you know when you have pushed the piece in the game that makes the tower fall? I fear you don't, and that's why being brave is not the absence of fear, but not allowing the fear to stop you.

Brave, in my experience, starts small and grows to another level. If it were a recipe, it might read something like this:

- One healthy cup of *I don't give a crap what anyone thinks.*
- A tablespoon of fear with a dash of *holy crow this might be a bad idea.*
- One large cup of humility and perhaps half a cup of *I can move to another town if this doesn't work out.*

How big is someone's brave and how do you find it? Baby steps and trial and error are all I surmise.

I asked my clients who wanted to do their first 5K run, 'How big is your brave?' After completing the 5K, they had the courage to be brave enough to sign up for the next distance race.

When brave is something you have a healthy respect for, along with enough curiosity to find out where the brave boundaries run, fear becomes less of the focus. Brave are those things that require deep breaths and sharp focus.

Often, you need cheerleaders and instructors to help you find your way. Sometimes brave is not pretty. I remember in my bodybuilding days not being called out in the top five finalists. But I was so certain I would be, I went out on stage anyway.

When I counted the finalists and realized I wasn't one of them, I remained on stage and laughed it off. I wasn't as embarrassed as I was feeling brave. I knew at that moment I would be the only one who remembered it once it was over, so why be embarrassed?

Brave can sometimes feel like the pitch changes in your voice when you try to say something profound and fear speaks first. My brave feels big, but with curiosity as my guide, I know it can be bigger. I love the way brave makes you feel, like a good friend who tells you how strong you are. Brave can give you better vision and a passport to a bigger life experience.

This is one story of what happens when you take on a new brave:

It was Wednesday, 4 November 2016 and I was driving to Panama City Beach, Florida, to finish what I started almost a year earlier. Susan, a fitness colleague and friend, was riding with me. We were now partners in a great adventure called the Ironman competition.

Begun in 1978, the Ironman is a grueling triathlon that challenges competitors to swimming, biking, and running for long distances. Events are held worldwide. Since the seventies, the number of competitors has grown from a mere handful to more than fifteen hundred athletes who now compete annually.

When Susan and I had met six weeks earlier, we never would have guessed we would be traveling partners, roommates, and fellow finishers. I told her it was divine intervention that we had encountered each other. She had completed more than a dozen Ironman races prior to this one, and I knew she would be a tremendous help to me.

I asked her a million questions about what to expect for this big, upcoming event, hoping she would be able to give me an inside perspective. *What was the hardest part of the competition? How best could I prepare? What made the difference between those who finished and those who didn't?* These were my pressing questions.

She took special care of me during this time, an Ironman "guardian angel" of sorts, and I felt as though her help would be the defining difference in this race.

Making things more complicated, my normal life as a trainer, wife, and mother had changed dramatically. I was in the process of a divorce. During this tumultuous time, I knew my Ironman training would suffer greatly.

For instance, I was forced to move three times from my house to a rental property, then to another rental house before moving back into my own house only a week before the scheduled competition.

Despite the disruptions in my personal life, my training was still important. But the time I could devote to it changed significantly. Sometimes, my training was limited to watching "how-to" videos from former Ironman athletes via YouTube.

I figured the visual training was better than nothing at all, and though I had trained for more than a year, I still needed more. Susan assured me I would be fine and that I had done enough training. Before long, I believed her encouragement created a shift in me—from fear to hope.

My close friend Kiki, who had helped me in the New Orleans half-Ironman, was the best support crew I could have, as well as my dearest friend. She had agreed to meet me later in Florida for the event. At least, I thought, I had a plan.

That would quickly change when Susan called me two weeks before the Ironman and said friends who had rented a house had space for me and Kiki. Not only would staying with other athletes be exciting, but it would save me almost six hundred dollars.

Not long after that, Susan asked if she could ride to the event with me. Just like that, my guardian angel was now my co-pilot. I was thrilled and at peace, as I knew my biggest obstacle was becoming a much smaller hurdle.

Susan and I agreed to leave on a Wednesday, giving us two days to prepare for the Ironman on Saturday. Traveling with someone, you never know what can become a challenge.

Will they need a pit stop every two hours or insist on numerous unscheduled stops?

Music inspires me while driving, but when someone else is present, I always worry about the station we will settle on. I like country music, but not everyone does. Three hours into our trip, I asked Susan if she could tolerate my favorite station.

To my relief, she said yes and then added, 'I'm so glad you like country music.'

We were soon laughing at the coincidence. We talked about everything in the next twelve hours, but at the same time, refused to lose focus on the upcoming race.

Although, Susan was an under fourteen-hour finisher (which is impressive for an Ironman competitor), she felt this particular race was one she was less than prepared to complete. She had just moved to Asheville from Michigan and hadn't been able to train diligently.

She was, she explained, working long hours at a running equipment store and trying to get settled into the area. She didn't know Asheville well enough to train the same as in her hometown.

I practiced convincing myself that I could be a finisher, too, and not allow Susan to feel or smell my fear when she mentioned that she was not as prepared as she had hoped.

Susan is a strong swimmer, and I asked her what she thought about the conditions of the water in which we would be competing. The year before, she told me, the waves were so high and the currents and riptide so dangerous, the swim was canceled.

For me, not to complete all three parts of the Ironman would feel as though I had not completed it at all. I hoped that would not be the case this year as I planned to swim, bike, *and* run.

Susan was a great travel companion, easy to talk to, easy to laugh with, and someone who didn't take herself or our sport too seriously. I began to feel more comfortable and closer to my dream every mile we drove.

I also began to realize that Susan and I were shaped the same—strong and solid—which made me feel more confident about my chances of finishing. A triathlete is often built leaner for speed, and although Susan wasn't fat, she was stout. Yet, she was also fast.

She had a number of friends in the triathlon world and said we would be staying with three of her friends, two of whom were triathletes, and one the wife of a triathlete. I was thrilled to be staying with other athletes, as I knew the camaraderie would be fun and helpful.

We arrived around dinner time, made introductions, and headed off to dinner together as though we had been friends for years.

Steve was a dentist from Michigan who had been doing Ironman races for a number of years. He was tall, thin, and bald, all things that lent to his quickness. His wife was his support crew and cheerleader.

Peter was an Australian living in the U.S. who also did triathlons but came only to watch this one and to help Steve and Susan if they needed anything. He was their support crew and became part of mine as well. In the beginning, hanging out with Peter was very helpful.

However, by the second day, I was in shutdown mode due to an overload of information from Peter. If I had met him a year ago, it would've been helpful. Unfortunately, I was meeting him two days before the event.

All the information he was giving me was too much and too late. Still, I thought, I can't turn back now. I had to soldier on and try to tame my anxiety, especially about the swim. I had never trained in salt water and was nervous about the 2.4-mile swim, one of the three parts of the Ironman.

Thursday morning, we put on our wetsuits and jumped into the sixty-five-degree salt water in the Gulf of Mexico. I had ordered my wetsuit earlier that month and had only worn it twice, both times in a lake.

It was exceptionally warm for early November and there was a great deal of discussion about whether it would even be wetsuit-legal. The Ironman determines suit conditions the morning of the event, roughly around four a.m. The temperature considered legal is seventy-six degrees or below. It's best to be able to wear a wetsuit because it allows you to be more buoyant and in turn, use less energy.

I stepped into the water, my heartbeat ratcheting up to match my fears. Breathing while swimming can be difficult enough, but adding fear makes it impossible to enjoy the day. The current was strong and made me a little nauseous.

Despite my best efforts, I couldn't get my breathing steady. I was hoping to break into a steady, powerful stroke, but it was a real challenge. Friday morning, we all agreed to meet and swim again. I was still not excited but knew I needed to keep trying in order to conquer my fear.

Friday was a much better day. I was certain by then I could do the 2.4-mile swim required as long as the conditions cooperated.

My dear friend and solo support crew, Kiki, arrived from New Orleans on Thursday evening. She was a breath of fresh air. She knew me well as we had tackled this team effort together before. She was as comfortable to me as a favorite T-shirt or pair of jeans. After she got there, I felt better in my skin and in my soul.

Kiki was detailed in her plan for supporting me throughout the events of each day. She said she was like a coach working with a star quarterback. She also gave me her opinions about the best plan for the day of the race. We spent much of Friday resting and getting ready until it was time to move toward check-in.

Since I was signed up under the organization which had sponsored me, I didn't have to stand in a long line of athletes to get my bags and information, my numbered shirt, and other goodies. They simply asked my name and handed me a number. Volunteers were everywhere, pointing to the next station.

Next up was what I referred to as the "gauntlet", a maze-like procedure that can test anyone's patience. First, you sign a waiver and then receive your transition bags—one for swim, one for bike, one for run, and two for special needs. You get a T-shirt and a sturdy backpack imprinted with the words *Ironman PCB2015*.

I worried I would miss a station, or forget gear or a number, or whatever I needed. Therefore, I went carefully through the maze, collecting my things and hoping I didn't miss anything. Just like Disney World, however, the line ended in the gift shop with Ironman gear everywhere. I felt proud to be there and participating, but still not brave enough to buy anything.

I was scared it might jinx me.

Triathletes are gear people. We have all kinds of gear that ranges from specialized food, clothing, tires, salt, glasses, and a million other things. There are vendors everywhere, counting on the fact that we would spend anything to be faster, more comfortable, or better able to enhance our chances of a finish.

I decided to rent racing wheels for my bike as I had heard time and again racing wheels can make all the difference. When you're on a bike for at least six hours, even an extra fifteen minutes can matter.

The bike wheels were installed by mechanics, but you always worry things can go wrong. If, for example, you get a flat tire, it can cost you lots of time getting it fixed. Peter was trying to help me by telling me I should learn to change the tire. Yet, I felt at that point it was pointless.

If I had a flat, I was almost certain panic would set in and I would be at the mercy of the road crew who, hopefully, would find me.

Then we stopped at the grocery store to buy healthy food for dinner. The rule was no carb loading, so most contestants consumed chicken, broccoli, and rice. The right food was critical because if you ate something that didn't agree with you, or if nerves got to you, the resulting assault on your digestive system could lead to real trouble.

I planned ahead for my normal breakfast that morning—oatmeal with blueberries and protein powder. Wake-up was at four a.m. and we were off to race point at four-thirty, even though the race didn't start till six a.m. Thousands of people have to get their equipment ready, and that takes extra time.

Before leaving the house, I took a few minutes of quiet time—just me and the waves in the darkness overlooking the beach. It was in that moment I thanked the Lord that I was allowed to enter this event. I thought of those who would have, but couldn't, and I thought about the message I hoped to give my children when it was over: *You can do anything you set your mind to. Just be brave.*

At the event, we were told it wouldn't be wetsuit-legal. In order to be wetsuit-legal, the water temperature must be colder than 76.1 degrees Fahrenheit. I decided I wouldn't wear mine even though I could have if I agreed to start in the back.

By now, my nerves were on point and my heart was thumping in my chest. I could hear the naysayers—those crazy, circus voices in my head—telling me I was insane to do this.

But, I walked to the starting line, overwhelmed with pride and joy, hushing all the voices in my head. The morning in Panama City Beach, just before sunrise, was windy but warm, and the waves began to look a bit dangerous. Their size and roar increased with every step as I got closer to approaching the starting line.

I ran the training over in my mind one last time and decided I had nowhere else to go. The water would be the most challenging event for me, as many elements were unknown. I also think the ocean is more challenging because of the salt water and the waves.

There is no land to use as a site or a guide. At least in a lake you have the land to help guide you, and the fresh water makes it easier to swallow if you accidentally intake.

The swim started without incident, but I still found myself struggling to get a good breath and a good rhythm. I was now swimming sideways, despite correction after correction, and was convinced I had completed the 2.4 miles.

At 1.2 miles I would have to exit the water and run to the beach, re-entering the water for my last 1.2 miles of the swim.

As I glanced at the clock, I knew I had only two hours and twenty minutes to get it done, or I would be pulled from the race and unable to continue. The waves had grown in size, and the second entry into the water would be far more difficult since I had just struggled the first 1.2 miles.

I knew I could swim and I knew I could go the distance, but that's before I saw the waves. The expanding waves were knocking people down and slinging boats from side to side like toys. I began to doubt my ability.

Quickly, the pep talks in my head turned to questions. *Can I really do this? Do I really want to do this?* It's amazing how quickly the power of perception that allows you to try most anything becomes the poison of perception instead, as in *I can't possibly do this.*

How big your brave is becomes the only thing you can use to scale the wall of fear and get out of the place that has you paralyzed, releasing you to do the most important thing you came to do.

Hesitating, I went over in my mind one simple reminder: *I didn't come here to quit. I came here to finish and I will, no matter what.* I remembered watching other athletes swim with challenges greater than mine—missing limbs that required they be pushed on a bike, pulled in a rescue boat, or encased in a wheelchair.

I thought of all the strong, resilient women I had trained and the many obstacles they had overcome, from physical infirmities to the sheer terror of self-doubt.

There would, I told myself, be no time for delay over fear. I completed the second 1.2-mile swim with ten minutes to spare. I ran through a quick freshwater shower, not giving much thought to washing all the salt from my swimsuit, an issue that would arise later.

I then ran into a large tent to grab my transition bag and all the things I needed for the bike ride, frantically getting ready for the next event. I needed to leave quickly, but be mindful that I would be on the bike for a hundred and twelve miles.

I had to make sure I had chafing cream in all the right places, make sure I was dry enough from the swim, and that my hair was pulled back in a tight, saltwater dreadlock kind of mess. I had sunglasses, sunscreen, a small nutrition bar for sustenance, and a whole lot of guts—ready to take on this next big challenge of my day.

Ironman races, because they are held in cities where traffic and people reside, must employ cut-off times so normal life and traffic can resume. The swim time is two hours and twenty minutes, the bike time seven hours, and the run time is eight hours for a total of seventeen hours.

No, I wasn't breaking any records, but I did feel the best while riding my bike. I decided early on in the race I would pay attention to the cut-offs, but enjoy the day, too, once I got on the course.

After seventeen hours, the race is shut down, but along the way if competitors aren't making the cut-off times, they are pulled off the route to avoid further delays. Many of us passed each other, making light-hearted jokes along the way.

In those moments, you get a feel for the people who are struggling and those who are going to finish strong, just by the looks on their faces.

The weather stayed clear for much of the day and the ride felt good. I waved at friends cycling by, noting as I passed mile forty if this were a half-Ironman, I'd almost be done.

However, in this race, I still had seventy-two miles to go.

Those miles allow you to think a lot, like what it took to get there and how many hours you spend on your bike. You think about why the race is important and most of all, what it will feel like to finish.

The bike was my favorite part of the Ironman and toward the end, I began to unclip my shoes, which had been clipped into the bike pedals for more than a hundred miles. I was nearly done with this segment of the race.

At the end of the bike stage, I slipped into my running shoes. I was now ready for the last phase.

It was when I started to run that the struggle became truly difficult. I had eaten a variety of things on the course to keep my fuel levels up, mostly peanut butter and jelly sandwiches, my favorite.

It was like being a child again, the sandwiches filling me up without causing an upset stomach. Thanks to the peanut butter, the protein snack prevented me from getting tired or distracted due to hunger.

The run would be the biggest beast of the event for me, even though I love to run. It's just that I'm a slow runner, which meant I would face all kinds of fatigue. The salt water had crystallized in my shorts and under my arms, making them feel like sandpaper. My skin rubbed against itself, and the sun baked my exposed arms and legs, despite my sunscreen.

I was now exhausted. But I still had seven hours left to complete a full marathon. My body started to revolt. About four-thirty p.m., I began to hurt. My head hurt most, yet my heart felt amazing. I was two-thirds of the way through completing the biggest dream of my life.

As I continued to run, it was hard not to cry due to an overwhelming joy. I had dreamed about this for twenty years, and now I might actually finish a full Ironman!

As I painfully took each step, I went over every detail of how and what it took me to get to this stage; the highs, the lows, the confidence, the doubt, the winning, and the losing. Before that day, I wasn't sure how big my brave really was, where the boundaries lay.

For years, I had wondered what I was truly capable of doing. I used stories I heard of how difficult it would be to keep myself from trying sooner than I did. I also found myself allowing my doubts and my prior failures to be barriers between my dreams and success.

This event, I realized, would single-handedly open up a new path, a new horizon, and a new vision of the future. I had used this experience to change the course of my life. And for that alone, I could be proud.

One thing didn't change, however—I knew I was going to finish. Once I made it to the marathon, even a painful walk would still get me across the finish line as long as I paid attention to the time.

I prayed my body wouldn't cramp. I watched people vomit and continue running, people stop and fall in front of me, their bodies on strike and their Ironman dreams gone.

Each step was like a thousand needles sticking into my feet. My knees hurt, my back hurt, and my head hurt. I felt almost like a shell of a human. But I was on fire for what I was doing.

Around mile six, I ran into my friend, Susan. When we met up, she was six miles from the finish while I was still fifteen miles away.

We fell into a running pace then slowed to a walk, talking and laughing about how we had made it this far. I was thrilled to see her, although she would separate from me on mile thirteen and finish her race in thirteen hours, while I continued on. I was grateful for the time I had with her.

I had purposefully left another pair of shoes at the special needs truck on mile thirteen. I wanted to change shoes, hoping it would help my feet feel better about the remaining miles. It was a peace offering to my feet.

While changing my shoes, I discarded a great pair of shoes knowing I would never see them again, anguishing over the ninety dollars I had spent on their purchase.

I looked toward the sidelines and spotted my friend and support system, Kiki, behind one of the barriers. I asked her if she had her running shoes on and explained that she would need to run the next thirteen miles with me, or there was a good chance I wouldn't finish.

She was all in, she said, her eyes lighting up. She knew that we weren't allowed to have outside help, but that "pacing help" was allowed for the athletes without the danger of disqualification.

During the next thirteen miles, Kiki followed along, pointing to the finish line, yelling, 'Jo, you have to keep moving your feet!'

'I'm going as fast as my feet will let me!' I yelled back.

In truth, I was physically exhausted, emotionally spent, with pain that had a voice separate from my own. But Kiki never gave up on me, running in the rain, smiling, and encouraging me every step of those last required miles.

She did this for me the entire day with little reward. Friendship and camaraderie are two of the reasons I picked this sport, and I couldn't have picked a better friend to help me get through it.

Another A-lister was one of the marshals riding a bike to keep us aware of the cut-off times, used by the race marshal and volunteers to know when someone was too far behind to finish.

This particular marshal had learned my name, and about every few miles she would circle back and say to me, 'Jolene, you didn't come here to quit.'

There were a few times I wished I hadn't told her my name, but she was part of my finish now and part of my Ironman story. Between my bike angel and Kiki, I knew I was unstoppable and that I would, in fact, finish this race.

I believe now that your body can hurt so much it feels like it might split open, your guts falling out with nothing recognizable left. Remaining is your head and your heart if you continue to believe that the finish is near and that you can do this.

I had witnessed firsthand the power of my perception, the reality I was creating to be an Ironman finisher. I had been able to craft the ending and simply follow the road I had carved out through hours and hours of training. True, it was touch and go, and sometimes I wondered if my positive thinking would be enough.

Those last few minutes in particular, I had grave concerns that I might not finish as we were told there were only twenty minutes till lights went off. Although, my feet were moving, it was like moving in mud. I was about a half a mile out, which seemed completely doable if I had not endured more than sixteen hours prior with the other events.

As I turned the corner, I could hear the roar of the crowd, see the lights, and suddenly realized, *I'm approaching the red carpet.*

I had been cautioned that the red carpet would be almost half a mile long and that I should reserve energy. But I wasn't worried. At this point, I knew I was closer than I had ever been to finishing my race.

From the corner of my eye, two neatly dressed gentlemen wearing jeans and lanyards appeared. They looked like press people or athletes who had finished the race, showered, and came back to cheer for the finishers.

As they walked toward me, one pointed at me and yelled, 'Do you know what's about to happen to you? You are about to become an Ironman. Raise your hands in victory and run through the shoot. Own every minute!'

I knew then what celebrities must experience when they approach the red carpet—flashes of lights everywhere, people screaming and trying to touch them. This was the closest, most celebrated moment of my life. I felt amazing.

The kind strangers who line the finish lines of Ironman races simply to give high-fives are also some of my favorite people. As instructed, I raised my hands for the shine of victory and ran through the finish line.

I cried and hugged my friend, Kiki, who like a stealthy soldier had made it to the finish line with me. I stayed on my feet despite how much they hurt. I was given my medal and like an Olympic athlete, I bowed my head as it was placed around my neck.

I was overwhelmed. I had done it. My words and beliefs had become my reality. I had actually crafted a dream and seen it through, allowing me to feel the scope of how big my brave was for this moment.

Within minutes, I heard the countdown and watched the lights go dark. I knew there were a number of people who, despite their best efforts, were still on the course and wouldn't finish. It's difficult to know you have done everything and still might not make the finish line.

In the moment, fear can paralyze you and keep you from doing something great. Fear can lie to you and tell you that you don't matter. Each one of those athletes had a reason for trying and a cause they supported and worked hard to sustain. Some finished and some did not.

But in the end, everyone out there mattered because they had overcome their fears and made the attempt, win or lose.

Making a difference in the world starts in your own heart, but making a difference in the lives of others allows your heart to connect and your fear to dissipate.

We all have hopes for the big things we want to do— some for our own heart and some for the hearts and journeys of others. But seldom do we get to attempt the "big things" that can—if successful—literally mean the difference between life and death.

Following the Ironman event, I was fortunate enough to be in the right place at the right time to do just that. Just as the Ironman changed me and my connection to others, this new, "big thing" is something I will never forget.

I could now take the power I had gained from changing my perspective about my abilities and use it to help save a life.

Chapter Ten
When Success Means
Life or Death

I have trained myself and others to believe that life is an athletic event and being prepared is crucial. You run from one life event to another, leap over hurdles placed in your way, and lift the heavy stuff in order to keep moving forward.

My friend, Jessica, is a perfect example of someone who ran the course, leaped the hurdles, and lifted the heavy stuff that came her way. She never knew how strong she was until being strong was all she had. When Jessica was injured in an accident and started her new life as a paraplegic, I was certain that if she had not been in such good shape, her recovery would have been much more difficult.

I often joke that I want to be that ninety-year-old woman on the tennis court hitting an ace and heckling the young sixty-year-old whippersnappers, but really, I have no idea if I will even get to be ninety. I work out with the hope that this long-term investment will pay off and every day I will be ready for what life brings me.

Interconnected is my desire to make a difference in the world. I think being healthy allows me to help when I am called upon. I see many people who struggle with whether they can get out of bed on their own every day. Others worry about how they look, what material possessions they "must" have, or what to eat next.

They are consumed by a life they are trying to live that may or may not be a healthy one. All I hope for is that I will be agile enough, healthy enough, and live long enough to make a difference in the world.

Part of the "how big is your brave?" journey requires a certain amount of trial and error. I believe some of us are tasked with more difficult trials than others, with some that seem insurmountable.

I also believe if we were handed a difficult task or trial and could refuse it, many of us would. That's because we think we have the ability to only handle certain tasks and certain trials.

The truth is, we really don't know what we can handle until it shows up.

I hoped to be challenged in life and accomplish what I first thought I couldn't. In 2009, I got my chance. While visiting Dallas a few years earlier, I had trained a client who worked in marketing at a major retail headquarters. I was a trainer in their corporate gym, and Sheila was one of my clients.

She was one of the first five clients I worked with after being certified as a personal trainer, and to say I was nervous was an understatement. A young woman, Sheila had long, gorgeous hair and wore makeup. She was stylish, trendy, and cool.

I felt lucky that I was her trainer. I had just had my daughter so I wasn't feeling super about myself, but I loved training others. Sheila and I worked together for several months and shared great times.

She had a golf tournament sponsored by her company coming up in a few months, and she wanted to practice swinging a golf club because she had never taken lessons.

I loved golf and had played since high school. I suggested we go to the driving range and hit some balls to practice. As we reached the green, I cautioned her to never stand behind me while I was swinging the golf club as it could be dangerous.

We practiced for a while and I could tell she was trying to kill the ball, so I took the club and said, 'Let me show you what you are doing.'

As I reared back to demonstrate the "killing it" motion, I heard her scream. I turned and, to my horror, found her not only standing right behind me, but holding her ear. I had hit her with the club where her earring was attached.

The club ripped off her earring and split the earlobe in two. As we rushed to the emergency room, I kept thinking this was the worst thing a trainer could do to a client. At least that's what it felt like to me. She probably felt the same. In fact, I worried that I had changed her entire perception of trainers with that one wild swing.

Four hours and a large bandage later—along with a warning not to play golf for a while—we were free. I then had to call my liability insurance carrier, explain the incident, and hope it was covered under my policy. I heard my claims representative trying not to laugh (he later said it was a hard story to believe) when I relayed what had happened.

Fortunately, my insurance covered her injuries. Sheila healed and we tried to return to normal training. I was relieved that I would be moving to North Carolina two months after that incident because it pained me each time I saw her. I felt horrible about the whole thing.

In addition, I wanted to give Sheila a new trainer following the incident, as most trainers don't try to kill their clients with a golf club (or anything else). I thought I was the worst trainer ever. What I didn't know then is that the bad experience Sheila and I shared would become something wonderful.

Over time, Sheila and I got to know each other well. Just before I left for North Carolina, she shared with me that her brother had been diagnosed with leukemia for the second time. I was sad for her and her family. This seemed like a tough fight because it was round two, and sometimes that can be worse than round one.

I told her after I moved, I would check on her and her brother. I did, calling them several times.

During one of our phone calls, I asked if there was anything I could do to help. She explained her brother was in need of a bone marrow transplant and required a bone marrow match. She asked me to consider being a candidate and joining the National Registry, though she explained it would be a long shot if I was a match for her brother.

Good matches are hard to come by, she said, and perfect matches are even rarer.

But to be a match to anyone would be a victory, she added. It was a crazy time in my life and, with two small children, life got away from me. It was October 2009 before I got around to registering.

I had since moved from Raleigh to Asheville and it had been almost nine years after she had made the initial request. Serving as a vendor at a health fair in Asheville, I was talking about my wellness services and personal training business to passers-by.

I was approached by a woman who was holding a plastic container with what looked like a long Q-tip inside it. She asked if I would consider being a bone marrow donor. I thought of Sheila's brother.

Without hesitation, I said, 'Yes. What do I need to do?'

She explained it was very simple. She swiped the inside of my mouth and placed the swab inside the container. 'Now all you have to do is wait,' she said. She assured me that many people are on the list and never get called. But I knew this wasn't as much about being a match as it was about keeping my word.

I felt relieved when I was able to complete the task, even though I knew that Sheila might never know. At this point, we had lost touch, but I felt it was part of putting things to bed and making good on my word.

In December of that same year, I received a call. Would I be willing to explore being a possible match? The odds that I could be a possible match in as little as two months were not lost on me.

I knew the timing was perfect when I was able to connect the dots. This process had started nearly a decade earlier—put into motion with the errant swing of a golf club.

I am always fascinated by the way things work out or show up. Many of us experience this when we meet someone we instantly like, and find that we have many things in common.

Some call this coincidence, some call it destiny, and some think nothing of it.

But I have always believed that the greater good in the world is working in our favor. This phone call would be part of a greater good, and I knew then that I would be a bone marrow donor despite the odds against it.

Once selected, the donor begins with an appointment at a blood center for a blood draw, after which the sample is shipped off to the lab for testing. It can be weeks before you know whether or not you are a match.

Meanwhile, mounds of paperwork arrive, explaining all the risks that are possible in being a donor. The procedure in 2009 was still very much the same as it is today, but more opt to use their own stem cells today in lieu of the bone marrow transplant. The cells are removed from their blood, cleaned, and infused back into their body.

Finding a bone marrow match can cost valuable time and oftentimes doesn't produce a match.

There are risks and there can be complications, which sound really scary, but I wasn't particularly worried. I recalled a favorite quote from the movie *The Best Exotic Marigold Hotel*: "Everything will be alright in the end…if it's not alright, then it's not yet the end."

I knew that due to all the things that had to be in place for this to happen, not only would I see it through, but I would also be fine.

I was, however, still experiencing some fear. If nothing else, it gives you reason to pause and consider if this is, in fact, a good idea. I had heard through several people that the testing was painful, but I figured it would be something I could do given how healthy I was.

I was thirty-five years old at the time, and felt the best I had in years. I had my blood drawn and it was sent off for testing. I knew that few people made it past this point because a "perfect match" is so hard to find. It may sound strange, but I never doubted that eventually I would be a perfect match. I believe God wants us in just the right place at just the right time.

A few weeks later, I received a thick envelope with details about the selection process. I had made it past the first process and would need to go to Winston-Salem Baptist Memorial Hospital in North Carolina and submit to a battery of tests.

The paperwork offered little information about the patient, but it did say it was a boy age zero, which meant he was a newborn. I could feel the tears and the tightness in my chest rush to the surface. As a mother, I could not imagine having to go through this.

I had two healthy, vibrant children and if either one of them were afflicted with cancer, I would be lost. I can't even imagine being faced with a seriously ill child.

I went over the paperwork repeatedly, hoping to discover something that would tell me more about the patient or their family. On a follow-up phone call, a caseworker carefully explained all the risks involved in the surgery. It sounded grim and scary as she was talking, but I knew in my heart that as a mother, I had no real choice.

Another mother needed me to help her, so I knew I would help without hesitation.

Nor could I imagine waiting desperately for a match only to be told the donor had decided not to proceed. I only half-listened to all the warnings so they would not sway my decision. I was happy to be able to do something that didn't require any particular talent or any qualifying factors, as in running a marathon or competing in an Ironman.

This would require no special degree or basic knowledge of any subject matter—just a sincere willingness to help. The good news arrived in the mail. That I provided a perfect match was God's doing, not mine.

Another three months passed before the procedure was scheduled. With the day fast approaching, I was cautiously optimistic. What I tried not to focus on was that although I was a perfect match, the reality was the bone marrow transplant might not work.

Graft versus host rejection is a fairly common issue and can be fatal to the patient. While the marrow acceptance rate is better from a graft, the success rates from this method haven't dramatically improved due to the lack of viable donors. The reality is, a bone marrow transplant isn't always the cure for cancer.

But even as a long shot, the odds are still in favor of the patient, and since a transplant is often a last resort, it's impossible to say no. I prayed throughout this process that Baby Boy Zero would be saved through my bone marrow donation.

To complicate matters, I had registered for the Nashville half marathon prior to being selected as a donor and was scheduled to participate at the end of April. My date for donation was on target for the middle of March. I prayed the baby would stay healthy enough to be ready.

I learned he had two health setbacks prior to the transplant. The clock was ticking.

Being in great shape helped me feel good about recovery and minimizing my own complications, but didn't make me feel invincible. This was one of those things you prepare for unknowingly; a fluke of fate that means you are either the right candidate or you're not.

It could have just as easily been the case that my health was poor, or I wasn't able to donate because I wasn't healthy enough. Broadening the boundaries of my brave made me realize all my strenuous training had put me in a position to experience and overcome far more pain than a shot in the hip. In other words, through my training, I had been increasing my threshold for pain.

While I had the "right" marrow, I would also need good health to support the donation. For me it was like using geometry in a billiards game. You take geometry in high school thinking, *when in life will I ever have to plot points?* Then you're in a game of billiards and you remember degrees and how to create just the right angle, which helps you make your shot.

Despite the fact that the procedure was not simple and painless, I knew I could do it, and was grateful. I continued my half-marathon training and was scheduled to donate one month before I ran in Nashville. But I had made a grave error—committing to teach at a large local event only a few days *following* my surgery.

I had agreed to do this event long before I knew I would be donating. My name and the class were on a flier that had already been distributed. I promised the event organizer that I would be there, and figured if I needed to, I could teach without moving around much. The truth is, I had no idea what to expect with my surgery and my recovery.

The day for the bone marrow donation soon arrived. I was instructed to arrive the day before my surgery, which was on a Thursday. The actual time would be determined by the patient and their location, none of which they could disclose to me.

Typically, you are provided with no details about the patient. Once the transplant takes place, the patient's family can decide if they want to meet you, but only after a certain period of time has passed.

The transporting of the marrow is pre-arranged, centered on the patient being ready to receive it. In my case, there was only a six-hour window to transfer the marrow from me to little Baby Boy Zero. You are not paid to donate as this could create a risk given that too many people would sign up because they might make money being paid like plasma or blood donations. But your expenses are covered.

That meant a nice dinner out with dessert. No alcohol, of course, or eating after midnight. My husband (we weren't divorced yet) accompanied me. He was supportive of my decision but not enthusiastic given the potential risks and adverse outcomes associated with the transplant we were warned about. He came because I wasn't allowed to leave the hospital without a chaperone, and was told I couldn't or shouldn't drive for a few days.

After taking a walk not far from the hotel, we picked a quaint little restaurant in the downtown area. While enjoying the meal, I began to feel the magnitude of what I was doing. I compared it to walking past a stranger choking and stopping to help. From one human being to another, how can you ignore the need?

I was certain some people did say no, especially when they heard and understood the risks, ranging from numbness in the site for months to possible paralysis. But I had enjoyed thirty-five full and very good years, hopefully with many more to come. Baby Boy Zero likely had no years ahead without this transplant.

I arrived at the hospital early the next morning and donned the 'fancy' gown with the opening that exposes your backside, adding warm, grippy socks to my attire. I filled out stacks of paperwork, all of which I only half-read.

Although I wasn't alone, I felt as though I were, simply because I had no way to influence the outcome. In a race, you can talk yourself through the event and tell yourself everything is going to be just fine. But here, in this situation, you have no control over the outcome. You just have to be willing to show up and hope for the best.

An hour prior to the surgery, I was administered the special "knock your lights out medicine" and was off to the operating room.

Before lapsing into oblivion, I asked the nurses to take photos of the surgery as I was curious about this process. She explained that I would be lying on my stomach with my hips propped up in order for the surgeon to insert what looked like a twenty-foot needle into the bone. It wasn't that long, of course, but it sure appeared to be as she held it up to show me. Thick and lengthy, it had to be large enough to penetrate fully, she explained.

Once the needle was in my hip bone, they aspirated the marrow and captured it in a bag that looked similar to a blood bag. I had agreed to let them take an amount larger than was needed for the patient so the lab could study what was unique about the make-up of my marrow.

It then occurred to me—I'm not only a donor; I'm a scientific anomaly!

I was told the procedure could take up to three hours. Drifting off, I asked the nurse to please bring me the marrow when it was over. I wanted to see it and hold it. I was afraid if I told her I wanted to pray over it, too, and pray for the tiny patient who was receiving it, she might have thought that I was already delusional from the drugs.

A few hours later, I woke up in recovery and all was well. The nurse brought me the marrow and I held it in my hands, praying it would make a difference and change this family's future. I had also written the family a letter and asked my caseworker to send it with the marrow.

I had carefully inserted my name on the documents, but she had crossed it out on the form to protect both parties' anonymity.

'Just tell them I hope this will help,' I said. I wished I could have been there in person, held a hand, and looked them in the eye to witness what a difference this would make. But I knew that was a selfish, "look-at-me" kind of thing.

Looking back, I believe that if I didn't have health and well-being on my side, I would have been very afraid. I knew fear kept people from registering; no doubt fear of the unknown. I settled my nerves by reasoning: very few people died giving bone marrow; I had three-plus decades of good years with my legs intact, if they no longer worked, I would figure it out; and most of all—I knew that the good Lord had crafted this day so nothing bad would come of it.

The Ironman competition had served only me and no others, and although I was proud of it, this was different. This was a chance to do something selfless for someone; a way to look back and realize that while few people might ever know about it, the effect could change numerous lives.

The entire event, from start to finish, was not about the giving. It was about the receiving. It was a life-saving exchange between me and Baby Boy Zero—a constant reminder that I could do something good in the world and make a difference. In that sense, it was a gift to *me* as well as to him.

And don't we all want to do something that makes a real impact?

Today, I have three things I can be most proud of: my two children and the bone marrow donation. These three things have provided me with greater purpose, even in the gym.

I no longer trained for a "perfect body" (okay, maybe a little). I didn't run because I loved it (though I like it a little). I did what I did so I could show up each day, game ready.

The change in my spirit, although subtle, was significant.

I knew from that moment on, whenever destiny tapped on my shoulder or whispered in my ear "You're up", I would be ready. I could fulfill the task.

You never know when your own race will start, or when you need to play defense or offense for others. Being healthy and taking care of yourself can be the best way to prepare. It's a confidence and byproduct of the task I hadn't expected, and for that I was very proud.

Following my donation, I had to wait twelve hours to go home. The grilled cheese sandwich I was served in the hospital that day ranks among the best I've ever had, and I was convinced it was another gift for doing what I had done. While I was munching it down, the doctor who took my marrow came by to check on me. He was of Japanese descent, short in stature and serious in demeanor, but very kind.

As he stood there lacing his fingers in a studious pose, he said, 'The hospital, they get reimbursement. The family, they get reimbursement. I hope God reimburses you.'

With tears in my eyes, I replied, 'I have two healthy children. That's my reward.'

Within a day I was back to normal and feeling fantastic. I was told I would need to be in bed for a few days to recover. Though tired and sleeping a bit more than usual, I felt great. In fact, I felt so amazing after my donation, I was embarrassed people were sending me flowers and food.

I taught the scheduled class on Saturday, on fire and ready. A few weeks later, I ran the Nashville half marathon and though it wasn't fast or pretty, I made it through. Once again, I knew that the life of wellness I had invested in had paid me back in dividends. My good health made a difference and allowed me to pass along its rewards by helping someone else.

In Jimmy Carter's autobiography, *An Hour Before Daylight*, he describes his life growing up on a farm in Rome, Georgia in the early 1920s. In part of the book, he writes about how his mother would often feed freed slaves from throughout rural Georgia who came by the farm, which in 1938 was not a safe idea.

The road near his farm would later become Highway 280, and he said there were a number of times that freed black people got off the road and came to the back door at his home, asking his mother for food.

She never turned anyone away, though she was surprised at how many people stopped and asked for help. Eventually, she was brave enough to ask how they knew it was safe in rural Georgia to knock on her door.

The answer: it was okay to knock on her door because of a mark that past travelers had made on her mailbox each time they left with a bellyful of food and safe passage on the road. Other travelers recognized this was a place where they could be fed and continue their journeys elsewhere to find jobs as free men.

After reading that excerpt, I wanted this to be my new drive in life. I wanted people to put a mark on my mailbox, signaling it was safe, and that I would help them. No matter what the situation might be, I could be counted on to find my brave and use it for the common good.

It's my belief that in life we all desire a mark on our mailbox—a way that people can recognize us. Not only do we have the capacity to be generous and kind, but we can also set off on a mission in life to serve others.

I've always hoped that through my business in fitness and my desire to help people finish well, a mark on my mailbox would be symbolic, letting people know I was here to help.

When we allow fear of the unknown, fear of pain, or any other fear to keep us from helping others, we forget how the lives of others are impacted by our decisions. I never want to find myself afraid to make mistakes, or not be able to help when I know that I can.

Fear can paralyze you and keep you from even trying, and then the day comes when someone yells across the parking lot or whispers in your ear, "How big is your brave?"

I seldom tell people about being a bone marrow donor to toot my own horn, but I do tell the story to help people recognize the need for matches that remain today. The most underrepresented groups are Hispanics and African-Americans.

If, after reading this chapter, you feel led to get involved, the organization I worked with is *Be the Match*. Its site will walk you through the process and help you get signed up. Many who sign up will never be called to give, but they can study the demographics of people who register and perhaps even further the task of curing cancer that we still have yet to figure out. You can find more information on their website: bethematch.org.

I hope you, too, can tell a similar story and change the life of someone you may never meet, answering the call you never expected.

Nine months after I donated bone marrow, I was contacted and told that my patient Baby Boy Zero had passed away. Like someone reaching into my chest and squeezing my heart tight, I couldn't breathe and could barely talk.

The caller tried to say something kind, but I couldn't be consoled. My marrow had failed this family and I felt terrible. Then I realized, the poison of perception can turn things on a dime. I had two choices: I could allow myself the ability to feel joy that the family had gotten nine more months with their son and be glad that I was able to provide a little hope, or I could focus on the failure.

Once again, a new lesson was learned. Sometimes we can do everything right and nothing changes.

Being brave doesn't guarantee a successful outcome, or the one everyone is expecting. Yes, a happy ending for this family and their young child would have been awesome. But my story was only part of their bigger story.

Being brave allowed me to step into my part of the story and do my part. The end of the story wasn't written for me or by me. I choose to believe that my part made a difference and that was all I could expect.

Sometimes we don't want to take a chance because we can't guarantee the outcome, but that's what makes the brave, braver. You do it no matter what the outcome because you may find that in the end, you are an important part of a much bigger picture.

Chapter Eleven
Using Bravery to
Overcome Shame

This may seem like a strange story to put into a book about health, wellness, and finding your brave. At first, it wasn't clear to me. But then it came into focus why this is an important part of this book. It's a story about shame and how to overcome the many fears that surround it.

This was my first lesson in learning that fear, shame, and self-loathing can be a poison that alters your perception of yourself. It becomes the place where you put off being your best self, stop taking care of your health, begin hiding in your insecurities, and essentially lose yourself until once more, you find the courage to step out of the dark.

My experience capitalized on my fears and gave me several chances to be brave. This one incident would define the years I spent trying to figure out how not to react to life, but to respond to it. This changed the course of my life forever. The shame I felt from the incident and the vindication afterward, allowed me to become a better person and a better friend.

Our shame, I found, can be used to shine a light on our greatest victories if we know what to look for.

It was through being arrested that I was finally able to be set free. Here's how it all went down:

In the beginning of my adult life, when I became the wife of an Army officer, I had no idea what I was doing or how to develop a script that might help me evolve into who or what I wanted to be.

Instead, I grabbed a script from the life I wanted and played it out as best I could.

I will be a fit, strong, and loving wife, I thought. *I will show my husband love by eating healthy, exercising, and blending into the wallpaper, supporting him and praising him for every action and good deed he accomplishes.*

It was only later that I learned I was designing my own prison. Decorating the walls with intention and expectation, I took up residence in this confined space I had made for myself. As a result, I spent years working on someone who was inauthentic, someone I could never truly be.

Many of my friends after high school went on to marry and settle down, creating lives that looked traditional and "right". I longed to be like them, even though I had spent my life living like a gypsy (Army brat life makes you feel that way) and dreaming of things that most people would never think about trying.

My plan was to move to Vietnam to work at a new Coca Cola plant as an English teacher for the employees. A friend and I had gone to Japan to get new visas to make the trip and it was there I met my future husband.

Everything changed after that.

I married in 1994 with the intention of being the "perfect" wife. I loved all things right and good. I went to church and loved the people I met. I made a number of friends in my short time in our first duty station in Germany, and I was prepared (I thought) for Army life.

Yet, early on in my marriage, I felt inadequate and that my level of fitness was lacking compared to my new husband. I hadn't been a runner, but wanted to be better at it because that was how he spent a majority of his time. He could run for miles while I could only run a mile or two.

I knew being healthy was important to him, and I believed I needed to be doing what *he* thought was important, so running became my "doing".

I had played soccer in school, which involved short sprint training, but long runs were not my strong suit. Nonetheless, I began to try long-distance running. For proper running shoes, the best I could do were cute white sneakers, and I ran in them until my lungs ignited and felt as though a fire were burning in my chest.

I was working on the script I had written for the "perfect" wife and I intended to put in the time necessary to make it work. I began showing up at the gym every morning to add yet another level of dedication to the script. My hope was that a healthy marriage would be the outcome.

My husband expressed his approval by telling me he thought I was losing weight, getting stronger, and looking better every day. This was good. I felt I was getting somewhere because a good, strong, disciplined wife makes for a happy marriage. Right?

Never mind that I was not being honest with myself. Nor was the level of work easy to achieve. Nonetheless, I was getting the "right" reward because I was pleasing my husband.

A few months into my committed workouts, one of my gym mates, an instructor, said that it was possible to get paid for teaching fitness. I hadn't been able to secure a job because there were so few jobs for military wives on or off the base. Besides, working with locals would require a higher level of the German language than I possessed. So, when I learned I could exercise *and* make money, I was all in.

I learned all the details required and began the certification process to teach aerobics. I had very little training in dance, so I knew my class would be heavier on the athletics. This was at a time when step aerobics was just beginning. I used my best skill set to guide the class, which included an outgoing personality and an easy ability to make friends.

I had no idea what a thirty-two-count beat meant or how it could help me teach better. But I knew if I smiled often and helped people exercise, laugh, and have fun, it would be a success. I maintained a positive, upbeat attitude and in time, it began to pay off.

However, I was still trying to figure out the balance of helping people, getting fit, and becoming the best wife I could be all rolled into one. It was tough not allowing the perception of "being perfect" to hem me in.

A crack soon appeared in my triple efforts. I was starting to realize that my journey, which included the "perfect" wife script, no longer made a lot of sense.

It would be an understatement to say my husband was an ideal military officer. He was flawless, one of those people who made everything he did shine. I was in total amazement of his "Midas touch" and couldn't figure out how anyone could be so perfect. I wanted that for myself with no signs of my former life where "messy but done" was the standard.

I wanted to be perfect and in perfect shape with the perfect life and perfect marriage. I figured if you worked hard enough, long enough, it could happen. I see it today in my fitness practice—young wives who come to me with the same script, hoping for the same perfect marriage and the perfect body with the fairytale ending.

I wondered if other women had adopted this belief because our parents seemed to have perfect lives. Perhaps the shows we watched growing up (like *Falcon Crest* and *Dallas*) gave us this impression that these versions of the world actually existed.

I believed at the time my script matched my husband's, and with the right amount of effort, I could be perfect, too, while supporting a military officer. My fitness life would transfer into my real life, I thought, and as I became stronger and fitter, I would become the ultimately all-around "perfect" wife, mother, and person.

It was not until years later I recognized the strength you gain is only in your own soul and your own journey, and that everyone's journey is different, including that of your spouse.

This led me to discovering Brené Brown's work on *Daring Greatly*.

Theodore Roosevelt's speech about the *Man in the Arena* is a part of her book that made an incredible impact on me.

He said, "It is not the critic who counts; not the man who points out how the strong man stumbles, or where the doer of deeds could have done them better. The credit belongs to the man who is actually in the arena, whose face is marred by dust and sweat and blood; who strives valiantly; who errs, who comes short again and again, because there is no effort without error and shortcoming; but who does actually strive to do the deeds…[with great] enthusiasm…[and] devotion."

The man, "who, at the worst, if he fails," said Theodore Roosevelt, "at least fails while daring greatly, so that his place shall never be with those cold and timid souls who neither know victory nor defeat."

My perception began to change as I took these words to heart and realized I had given the power of my journey to someone else, in effect making them responsible for my success. I have since discovering that lacking authenticity affects your path adversely and your efforts will be thwarted at places crucial in your growth, reminding you that you are off track.

My derailment occurred in the spring of 1994. Traveling was a way of life for Army families living in Germany. Budapest was on our travel list and rail travel was how we got around. Though Budapest is a wonderful, lovely city, traveling during that time could be risky.

In order to keep our money or passports from getting stolen, I had placed mine in a document holder held around my neck then stuffed inside my shirt. We traveled back from

Budapest by train on a Sunday night and arrived home late. I laid my document holder on the nightstand and went off to bed.

Still true to my script, I woke up at my normal five a.m. time to get to the gym in order to fulfill the life I was sketching out for myself.

Exhausted from our trip, I was rushed, running late, and unknowingly left my identification on the nightstand. I jumped in my car and headed off to the gym, located on base.

When you arrive on base at six a.m., you are greeted by the sound of a bugle. This reverie alerts you to the day's start. Reverie comes from the French word "to rise", and it was mandatory that when it played, you stepped out of your vehicle, placed your hand on your heart, and waited for the seventeen seconds it took to finish.

Oftentimes the flag was raised, so standing at attention was a way to pay respect. Despite running behind that day, I was caught off-guard by the sound of reverie at the gate. I exited my car to pay proper respects.

Once it was over, I jumped back in my car and held my seat belt manually rather than clipping it in place. I was close to the gym. Surely a quick ride holding my seat belt would be fine.

As I pulled into the parking lot of the gym, I noticed a green army van behind me with the lights on, similar to police cars. It was an MP van—the military arm of the police. A young soldier approached my car and said he had stopped me for not wearing my seat belt. He explained it was a violation and that he needed to see my ID.

It was then that I realized I had left my identification documents at home. Now I had a tad bigger problem on my hands in addition to a simple seat belt violation.

I attempted to explain my situation and how I had left my ID at home after traveling, etc.

'Could we work this out?' I asked. The MP wouldn't budge. Soon after, my husband, who had driven to work separately and was contacted about my situation, approached the MP—a subordinate in rank to him.

'What's the problem, soldier?' My husband asked. Those with military experience understand this is often a subtle way of putting someone in their place. I knew then things were likely to get even worse.

I began to interject myself into the conversation again, this time trying to explain how such a minor issue had come about and that a ticket would not be a big deal, yada, yada. In fact, I said I was happy to take the ticket and be on my way. I knew it wouldn't result in a fine or serious consequences off-base, as military police power is limited.

Worst case, I would be placed on a list distributed daily of people who had violated traffic rules, and thought that meant I might risk shame on my husband by his military commander.

I told the officer and my husband that once I had the citation in hand, I would be done. So my husband headed to the gym and the soldier began writing the ticket. I was at the car retrieving what paperwork I needed when I noticed another MP van pulling in behind the first one.

A strapping, six feet two soldier with a large head, broad shoulders, and powerful hands approached me. Without warning, he shoved me into the car door, screaming in my face, 'Get in the car, ma'am!'

The incident was fast, furious, and caught me completely off-guard. I have been called a wild child and other names in my life more times than I can count. But never had a man I didn't know, and with no reason, push me aggressively with such force.

If anger were a speedometer, I went from zero to a hundred M.P.H. in an instant. Fear was my initial response, followed by surprise and anger. It was off to crazy town we went as I screamed at the top of my lungs, 'Don't you ever f%&*ing touch me again!'

I was waving my arms and in what felt like slow motion, the whole incident blew up. The MP Sergeant spun me around, slamming me into the car. Grabbing my hands, he placed them behind my back, snapped on the handcuffs, and had me in the MP van headed to headquarters before I fully realized what had just happened.

I could see the expressions on the faces of people passing by, who were going to the gym, as they witnessed my humiliation. I got looks of utter amazement that 1) something like this could happen before coffee and doughnuts and 2) that a woman could go from normal to a caged animal in a matter of seconds.

The ride to the holding facility felt endless. I went over and over the incident, my skin flaming red from embarrassment and anger, my heart pounding like never before. I could hardly believe what was happening. I suddenly went from anger to shame. Here I was, an Army officer's wife in handcuffs headed off to the D-cell.

I would be laughed at and gossiped over, not to mention the military ramifications that would befall my husband. Oftentimes, soldiers, and officers in particular, were rated on their job performance. Yet I also knew secretly—and not so secretly—they were rated on how their wives behaved, too. This entire incident was not good for me or for him.

How could I be the "perfect wife" now?

Deep inside, I felt a shift. Maybe I wasn't cut out to be a military wife, at least not one that required perfection. Maybe I wasn't cut out to be a military wife at all. I only knew for certain that I was now not only out of my comfort zone, but I was in what felt like a war zone, one of my own making.

I was processed and placed inside the D-cell, charged with not wearing a seat belt. It felt ridiculous; I was not a hardened criminal. It was just me, Jolene, the woman who wanted to make a difference in trying to get to the gym. Shock was another word that came to me shortly after the anger began to subside.

The protocol was to release the detainee (me) to a responsible party (my husband), but the soldiers in charge felt the release needed to be one rank higher, which meant his boss would have to sign me out.

In the end, this was all part of military posturing. There were no long-lasting consequences short of a conversation with my husband about how to behave. No charges were filed, no court date set, and no criminal record.

What followed the incident was shame, a stinging pain I continued to feel. I was released to my husband's commander and placed under strict orders to head home *pronto*.

Shaking with equal parts fear and anger, I went straight home and hid, closing all my curtains and going into a dark bedroom to cry and lick my wounds. An hour before, I was in handcuffs and headed to the D-cell. Now, I knew I would be labeled as a troublemaker.

It's true I was disappointed with myself. Why couldn't I have just relaxed when he pushed me? Why did I have to get so upset? A dear friend at the time brought me flowers and tried her best to make it a non-issue, but even she couldn't deny this wasn't a good situation for me or my family.

Later, when my husband came home, I could feel his disappointment and his uncertainty of what might happen to him. I knew what happened to me was wrong, but didn't feel as if that mattered much in the big picture. Conformity was standard in his world, and I had broken every link in the chain.

I spent the next two weeks hiding at home. I walked my dog in the vineyards behind my house and lay low to avoid any more incidents. I was beginning to shrink to my circumstances, and I was worried that my nature wasn't the right one for my new life.

I thought, I may be wild, but I may have no choice other than to stick it out now that I am in this place of shame.

My fear was beginning to win and keep me from doing what I needed to do because I felt the whispers were no longer whispers and that, in the end, I was a bad human. It paralyzed me and made me wonder if I was worthy of this life I was living.

Was conformity better than strife and disappointment? I was starting to believe the choices others made were far superior to mine, and I couldn't be trusted to make good decisions. I had built prison walls that would take me on a thirty-year journey of second-guessing myself.

I began to wonder if I should be supervised in life and could I actually be good at life without outside help. The truth was, I didn't feel worthy of having a voice and wasn't sure how to use it. Could I be brave enough to challenge the beliefs I had borrowed, challenge myself, and climb the walls of the prison?

This incident, now long past, but one I've never forgotten, helped me begin my journey and shaped me into who I am today. I realized shame and fear are powerful tools you use against yourself and can keep you from doing what you need to do to be yourself.

I also realized I would need to begin again if I were going to succeed. This was an opportunity, not a tragedy. In defiance, I began riding my bike six miles from my house to the gym. It would be difficult to arrest me for not wearing my seat belt.

I had just begun my journey to being healthy and I was working on getting certified to teach. I needed to be back in that gym.

And I needed to find myself once more.

I couldn't let fear keep me from doing what I was supposed to be doing. I knew most of the people in the gym, and of course tried my best to be light and laugh off what had happened, but that, too, was a hurdle. However, I was not going to be deterred from my goals. There was now a street fight inside my head and I would need every ounce of tenacity to get past it.

In the days that followed, the two MPs who had stopped me began harassing us. They followed my husband when he went on base and then made calls to his commander, claiming he was speeding or not following regulations. It was playground bullying, only with more severe consequences.

The military police are vital to all military bases, but sometimes you can find a soldier drunk with power who just isn't a good person. Because the military holds its own court, fear is used as a deterrent. My husband and I put up with the abuse for a few weeks, afraid to make waves and create more trouble.

About a month following the incident, we had to attend a large formal military function and knew the entire cadre (upper management) would be at the event. I also knew the wives of high-ranking officers would be there chatting and socializing.

I thought this might be a good time to let someone know what had happened to us without "reporting" it, and see if we could get a final resolution that would allow us to move past it. Being a military brat, I knew that wives had the ears of their husbands, and if you were coy enough, you could get things handled quickly and in a more efficient manner than through protocol.

All dressed up in military blues and formal dress, we had a wonderful evening out, and I was feeling more confident that our "Seat Belt Gate" might not ruin our military tour after all.

But I wasn't ready to let it slide.

I went to the ladies' room and noticed the commander's wife at the sink as I walked in. She was a lovely woman with a kind heart—a nurse and the mother of three children. I knew my story would not be lost on her, but I also knew I had to be brief. I quickly explained what happened, with few details, adding that it could happen to any officer's wife who came onto the base.

She looked at me and said, 'You mean you were arrested for not wearing your seat belt?'

I nodded, knowing she got it. And for the first time, I heard how ridiculous the whole thing sounded. I had allowed shame and discomfort to keep me stagnant and afraid. I was fearful of what people would say and think about me instead of realizing that worrying over what others think is always a no-win.

The commander's wife was both upset and appalled. On the Sunday night following the military function, the commander called me at home. He asked me to recite my story and said he would handle it from there. It *was* handled and we were vindicated. The MPs were reprimanded and told to leave us alone.

What couldn't be fixed was the time I had spent trying to fix myself and trying to make sense of the broken parts in me that made me a "criminal". I knew I wasn't really a criminal, but at that time, I wasn't sure how to make sense of it, and so I needed to feel guilty in order to resolve it.

What I needed to learn was how to be brave, despite what other people thought. To this day, I remain grateful for this incident. It has become part of my life story.

I learned in this moment and through this incident that fear will always be with us. It's how we use it that matters. Fear keeps us from jumping off cliffs and driving faster than we should. It keeps us from robbing banks when our funds get low, or going to jail when we want to break the law.

Fear even helps us stay fit by convincing us we must "look good" to "be good". In fact, some say fear is among our greatest motivators in every aspect of our lives.

But fear also keeps us hidden from our best self, keeps us from speaking up when something isn't right, and keeps us from taking time for ourselves or being selfish when we need to put ourselves first.

Fear can keep us from living our best lives and can cost us moments, years, or a lifetime. When you want to change, grow, or see yourself in the best light possible, fear will join you and dare you not to move. And it is fear that feeds the part of perception which can imprison us.

Completing an Ironman was accompanied by fear walking ahead of me. Bodybuilding and competing allowed fear alongside of me. Remaining stuck in a place for more than half my life was fear behind and within me. Fear can help you move to the next place, or it can paralyze you.

Life is designed with situations that can teach us and move us out of our comfort zones. It gives us an invitation to a much bigger, better, more authentic life, but it asks of us one thing—to take the risk. The risk requires that you be all in.

This means that the results can be what you expected or nothing you could have ever dreamed up. Sometimes we will be "kind of" in, giving it a half effort and then wondering why the lessons show up again. If we want to learn what life has for us, we have to show up and be all in. I am learning to do that today.

Sometimes, the lesson comes in a way we least expect it to. I was given a horse a few years back. He had never been loaded before and he wouldn't get on the trailer, even though we tried for hours to move him. He wasn't officially my horse yet, so I was a little tentative about trying to force him. After several hours of unsuccessful attempts, the owner called a horse trainer friend and asked for his help.

This man showed up in overalls, roper boots, and a long whip with a grocery bag tied to the end like a kite. He waved the whip behind the horse back and forth several times but never touched the horse. Before long, he had the animal moving from side to side in fear and then like magic, the horse jumped on the back of the trailer ready to head to his new home with me.

I was amazed and asked this experienced horse trainer how he managed the animal so easily.

'Ma'am, my job wasn't to make him get on that trailer,' he said in his heavy Southern accent. 'My job was to make it so uncomfortable he had nowhere else to go.'

It's up to you where you will go, how you will use fear to guide you, and whether or not you are determined enough to find your best life despite any obstacles that come your way. Fear, as I said in the opening pages of this book, can challenge, change, or crush you.

Are you ready to examine your faulty perceptions, escape from your self-inflicted prison, and put your fears to rest?

Life is our teacher. When the student is ready, the teacher will appear. What lessons have you been learning? What have you been avoiding? What keeps popping up in your life over and over that you thought you had addressed?

I have turned to fitness all my life as a way to learn about and challenge myself and it's helped repeatedly to show me how to use discipline to succeed. It may not seem the most obvious, but it has become the most resourceful way to challenge my beliefs and make new inroads to success.

Running solitude and biking solitude have given me a place to sort out things when clarity was an issue. Strength training gave me the courage to know when things are heavy, they can still be moved. Core training taught me that balance and the strongest parts of who we are require the most attention.

Yoga and flexibility taught me to be pliable even when I felt if I would bend, I might break. I have felt that my fitness journey was a chance for life to teach me without hiding from it.

I went looking for the lessons and the growth that fitness would teach me. I wanted to challenge life with my circumstances and my goals. Perception is something we can form to create good or bad. I have learned the bad will come, but the perception can be changed or created to become a positive.

I love the answer to this question someone once asked me.

'Is the glass half full or half empty?'

I responded in my optimistic way, 'For me the glass is always half full and refillable too.'

Then he said, for him, it depends on whether you are drinking or pouring. Such is the power of perception.

Chapter Twelve
Overcoming Fear of Aging

According to a MetLife Market Research Study conducted in 2003, baby boomers made up twenty-six percent of the total population. Baby boomers are men and women born in the years from 1946-1964. By 2017, the percentage had dropped slightly to 24.3 percent, but the overall sixty-five-plus population is projected to double by the year 2030. That's because people are living longer and healthier lives.

The past century has brought significant change in the aging process. Not only are people living longer, they are earning more, are better educated, and are far more active than previous generations.

The fitness industry has struggled with this rapidly growing generation of boomers. Classes were not initially designed for balance training, core strength, or education on long-term health benefits vs. weight loss and muscle building.

Many of the older population were showing up in gyms needing training, but had little or no guidance from trainers who knew how to work well with an aging population. Silver Sneakers became a popular class and at its peak accommodated the less agile baby boomer.

CrossFit and Body Pump seemed to be too much, causing concern for potential injuries, which seems counterintuitive to getting healthier and building muscle.

I recognized right away this would be a great group of people to work with and started fairly extensive research in what skills our aging but relatively fragile population would need.

I was excited about the possibilities of helping people who needed and wanted to live longer and more independently. Though I began the journey fearful of having enough knowledge and expertise to do the task well and determined to "do no harm", I wondered if I had the skills to make a lasting difference.

Using my ability to learn things quickly, I chose to dive right in. When I say dive in, I mean it took roughly five years as a trainer and several certifications to reach this goal.

My first (and to this day favorite) client was Valentina. She was a robust Italian woman who loved her family, her red sauce, and good red wine. She wasn't obese, just a little pudgy around the middle. "Fluffy" more than fat, she looked amazing at fifty-eight.

She said she had high cholesterol and high blood pressure issues and wanted to attempt to change the course of her life through fitness. Valentina, whom I nicknamed Tina, wanted to work together two days a week to help improve her numbers at her next follow-up physical.

Annual physicals are earmarks of good health after age fifty-five.

I was thrilled to help her and since time (she was retired) was no issue, I could work with her later in the mornings.

We worked together for almost three years, during which time I learned a great deal about Tina, her family, and her fears.

I discovered her husband had been diagnosed with Parkinson's and needed her to be in good physical shape in order to take care of him as the disease progressed (that was her explanation). She'd be able to lift him and assist him with walking if he got to the point where he couldn't do it himself, she said.

A retired physician, he was in the early stages of the disease and had conducted his own research, as well as gathered support from the medical community. Tina wanted to make sure she was up for the task and was always ahead of the game.

She worked hard when she showed up, sweating heavily, so she took to wearing a headband and bringing her own towel; full speed ahead. She wasn't afraid to try anything and oftentimes seemed to outwork my younger clients.

She amazed me with her can-do attitude, her grit, and her tenacity, inspiring me during each session. When she turned sixty, I was so proud to be her trainer and friend, I hosted a surprise birthday party for her.

As much as I was enamored and inspired by Tina, I also knew the industry would have to step up its game to meet the needs of the baby boomers. They weren't, I had learned, all fragile seniors who checked out large print books from the library, or took breaks from sewing circles to walk in the local mall.

Many of these folks were like Tina, bad asses raring to go and we would need to be ready. Because of the gap in the industry and the needs of people in that group, I found accommodating this population would take time, simply because no two boomers were in the same physical condition.

Part of being brave is facing our own mortality. I quickly recognized that many of the baby boomers I met had worked hard in their professional lives. Sometimes their health suffered greatly by the time they reached retirement.

Others had the comfort of financial means but were too banged up to enjoy it. I watched some who had waited until they retired to get in the best shape of their lives, but were too tired or unmotivated to make any significant changes, using the "can't teach old dogs new tricks" line as an excuse not to get involved in physical fitness.

***

While living in Dallas, Texas, I was asked to work with a woman named Leslie who had suffered a stroke from a blood clot that had traveled to her brain and ruptured. She had survived an embolism, leaving the left side of her body paralyzed. Making matters more challenging, she was part of the Tall Texans Club and was over six feet tall (the requirement for a woman in the Tall Texans Club) towering over my five feet four frame.

She asked if I would help with her rehab by doing yoga with her, I had little to no knowledge about strokes and had just been certified for yoga. I felt I wasn't the right fit given my shortcomings.

But Leslie assured me I could learn about the effects of the stroke and yoga, at whatever level I thought would be sufficient. I began attending therapy sessions with her and discovered the effects of a stroke on the brain, how resilient the brain is, and how one can even fully recover from a stroke.

I learned about the vitality in balance training and how helping older clients work on balance can create the same type of brain stimulation similar to rehabilitation in a stroke victim. I then used this in my work with the boomer population, adding balance and core training to all protocols, no matter the age.

Leslie and I did yoga together, though she struggled with muscle fatigue. With her progress slowing down, I came up with an idea to create a yoga weight combination called YoWei. It would allow Leslie to do yoga, but added five-pound weights shaped like grapefruits she could hold in her hands.

Even though her left hand was constantly closed in a grip due to the stroke, we found she could open her hand and fingers for therapy. But her hand quickly returned to the closed position.

She could wrap her hands around the weights during yoga, which helped build muscle and allowed her to gain more benefits from the yoga.

Fast forward almost six years later. Leslie and several of my older clients—including my Italian friend Tina—found that when they needed to work on building bone and muscle yet didn't want to give up yoga for weight training, they could have the benefits of both through Yo-Wei.

While training Leslie and Tina, I gained more confidence and worked with a growing number of senior clients. Several stand out in my mind, but the stories I share here are among the most notable.

***

Dennis saw my ad in the local paper for a boot camp I offered three days a week at the local community center. He called to find out about the classes and asked if I had room for an "old geezer".

I politely responded, 'Only if an old geezer has room for us.' I had learned by that time that you only get out of it what you put into it. I knew if you showed up and did your best, you would always get something from it. Age made no exception.

Dennis arrived and appeared to be a much younger "old geezer" than I had first imagined from his phone call. At sixty-three, he could do laps around nearly everyone, and although, he didn't lift the heaviest weight in the class, he showed up and showed out most consistently.

He only missed classes when he had to travel. I would later learn that Dennis was a television personality working as a product spokesman, oftentimes appearing on *Good Morning America* or the *Today* show, all of which he brushed off as just a job.

His work ethic and his leadership style made everyone want to work harder and up their game at boot camp.

Later, his wife joined us and the group flourished for more than two years. Then I took a position running a Wellness Center and found that in order to be at work in the mornings, I had to give up boot camp classes. I hated giving them up because these classes—and these "old geezers"—filled my soul with gratitude.

Dennis began to work out at home and started running. He and I met on a run one afternoon, and he told me he was competing in the Senior Olympics and had medaled in the regional competitions.

He had an infectious smile, a dope soul, and a deep desire to continue bettering himself. This, I felt, was the way I, too, hoped to grow old, loving every minute of it while inspiring others.

***

Judy was also a boot camp attendee. She had heard and seen Dennis in the class and knew she could do it as well. She was a wife, a grandmother, and a retired teacher who worked in a local bookstore. She was also an avid knitter.

She was, simply put, the coolest, and wore these great eyeglasses with black circular frames that gave her the perfect hip look, topped by a stylish short haircut that made her white hair look as though she were wearing a white mink hat.

I found her beautiful, funny, and kind. Life, it seemed, had been good to her overall. Like many women experiencing menopause, she had some excess weight in her midsection. She told us that menopause should be best described as a "mental pause" when your body and brain separate and your body becomes the "Wild West" with no sheriff.

However, Judy wouldn't let that stop her. Despite a bad knee, a hip that needed to be replaced, and her advancing years, she never showed up with less than her best. She did yoga, walked, and joined us for boot camp workouts twice a week, keeping it up until our class ended.

I can still see her smile, feel her zest for life, and hear her great belly laugh.

***

Bronnie Ware is a palliative care nurse who wrote *The Top Five Regrets of the Dying.* In her book, she describes what her patients reveal as they are leaving this world. Their regrets, in order of relevance were:

1. *I wish I'd had the courage to live true to myself, not the life others expected of me.*
2. *I wish I hadn't worked so hard.*
3. *I wish I'd had the courage to express my feelings.*
4. *I wish I had stayed in touch with my friends.*
5. *I wish that I had let myself be happier.*

These were heavy things to contemplate, but for the living are never too late to work toward. Taking your health back is one of the things that touches each of these regrets.

If your health isn't good, you can't travel to see the friends you still have. You can't enjoy life if your health is in shambles. If you are sentenced to a life of feeling bad because your body is tired and may be in the final stages of giving up, being happier can be a challenge.

I learned important life lessons from others I had trained. Many of my clients I had helped in turn helped me take a deep breath and appreciate each moment I could still enjoy.

My oldest client was seventy-three and a total spitfire. She said her boot camp instructors would take it easy on her, but she wanted to be whipped into shape. She had married a younger man and wanted to be able to keep up with him. After trying to find a way to close my jaw at the complete awe of her, I was elated to be her trainer.

We got together once a week, and she would always start the session with, 'Now, don't go easy on me.' In the beginning, I couldn't imagine putting her through the paces that I used with other younger clients. I thought I had to learn what she was capable of and then adjust.

But Martha challenged everything I thought that seventy-three looked like and was capable of doing. In fact, there was very little she couldn't do. She could pick up twenty-five pound dumbbells with ease that my thirty-something clients had lifted earlier that day.

I knew when things became challenging because she would close her eyes tight and wince to get the work done. At no time, however, would she quit or give up. Her tenacity was noteworthy and honorable. Her balance, as with many people her age, was poor, and she hated doing exercises that required standing on one leg or being on an uneven surface, but she would do them anyway.

I explained that independence requires you to be able to get up off the ground when you fall down, or not to trip, which could lead to a hip breaking at that stage in life. She would comply and shared how she had wished she had done more balance training in her younger years.

Balance training is a critical part of living a long life, not just in fitness training, but as a general rule. We know we need to work hard, play hard, and take time for ourselves to be truly balanced.

Balance training requires being in an unstable, unpredictable place and finding our center, our north, in the body and in life. Balance is also something we can have only through conditioning and practice.

As we grow older, our brain communicates less and less effectively with our body. The base of the brain is the cerebellum, which is the "power cord" from brain to body. It determines the effectiveness of the communication system, speed, and locations. The only way to keep the cerebellum sharp is through balance training.

When I had worked with Leslie after her stroke, one of the rehab exercises was to spin in a chair several times, then stop it. My job was to focus on her eyes and see how long it took her eyes to stop dancing. This challenged the body to bypass bad parts of the brain cut off by the stroke and make new ones so she could regain her balance and the use of her side that had been damaged from the stroke.

Balance and its training can make people uncomfortable. In my experience with clients, the more controlling they are in their personalities, the more they tend to dislike balance training. It requires them to allow the body to work on their behalf and give up control, allowing the muscles to make mental notes of where stabilization is occurring.

I have always found it interesting that being willing to let go and see what happens is a life skill, not just a fitness skill. Interestingly, the physical application and the emotional application are the same. The more unpredictably you train, the more prepared you are when life becomes unpredictable.

I loved working with my young-at-heart clients who came in weighed down by sweat, tears, a full life of family and loved ones, long careers, and yet still had the willingness to keep their minds and bodies sharp.

My industry may not adequately accommodate the aging population as well as it should. But when it does, the results can be spectacular for those who are brave enough to get involved and do their best.

Some boomers look phenomenal at seventy and some look feeble at sixty. The power in the perception of aging is that you are only as old as you feel, while the poison of perception is that when you are old and frail, it's too late to take back your health.

I would argue it's never too late to take back your health. There will be a surcharge on the use, but the return on your investment will far outweigh the consequences of not taking care of yourself.

Health experts agree. A recent twenty-year study conducted at the University of Cambridge and published in the British Medical Journal found that even a small amount of physical activity can boost life spans. Researchers found that with nearly 15,000 residents in the U.K., ages forty to seventy-nine, those who maintained or ramped up their level of activity from low to medium were twenty-eight percent less likely to die than those who maintained a low level of activity.

Low-level activity is defined as less than hundred and fifty minutes per week according to the World Health

Organization (WHO). Higher levels of staying active (defined as three hundred minutes of moderate-intensity weekly activity) achieved a forty-two percent increase in survival compared to the low-level group.

The results held even when the study's participants ate unhealthy diets or had chronic conditions including high blood pressure, high cholesterol, or were considered obese.

***

Tina and I see each other from time to time. She is still radiant, still moving, and still shaking it like no other woman I know. Leslie and I lost touch after I left Dallas. Dennis won all the medals he could and went back to working out for fun with his wife in their home gym.

Martha joined a boot camp program along with her forty-five-year-old son and his wife.

She continues to have the most drive and best attitude ever. She was able to complete the Cooper River Bridge Run in Charleston, South Carolina one year, and continues to make goals for herself.

I can only hope that my body will continue to make Judy-kind of strides as I age. Judy now cares for her husband as he ages with Parkinson's disease. She still does yoga, takes long walks, and belly laughs.

Life is short. We hear it all the time, but it can be longer—and better—if we are willing to make the attempt to recapture our health. Meeting the challenges life will throw at you, regardless of age, is one of the best gifts you can give to yourself.

Is your brave big enough to set aside your fear of aging and go for it? Are you willing to head to the gym to learn a new skill that might just prolong your life? Putting yourself first, no matter how old you are, is a fine place to begin.

Chapter Thirteen
Brave Hearts

Clients often asked if cardio was effective in weight loss. I told them cardio is good for your head and your heart. When the treadmill monitor screen displays that you have burned more than six-hundred calories, you think, "Wow, now I can eat a big dinner or have dessert. I burned a lot of calories!"

If only that were true.

Ironically, cardio is the least effective means for weight loss given its function because the calories you burn are usually the natural energy your body expends. It's called glycogen, not true fat burning. The good news is that the benefit is greater than that of weight loss and should be given a little more credit as its good for your head *and* your heart.

I am fascinated by the heart's complexity and, conversely, its elegant simplicity.

Symbolic of nearly everything we know about life; the heart is astounding in its design.

It only weighs between eight to twelve ounces, with a male's heart weighing slightly more than a female's. It's about the size of your fist, located in the center of the chest, slightly to the left. Since it has its own electrical system, it can still beat even when separated from the body. On average, this powerful muscle beats more than 100,000 times a day, pumping more than two thousand gallons of blood throughout the body.

Though no one truly knows why, statistically you are more likely to have a heart attack on a Monday, and more often on Christmas Day. What's not disputed is that heart attacks are the number one killer in women and men worldwide.

The American Heart Association, which contrary to popular belief does not conduct research (it funds research projects), reports that cardiovascular diseases (CVD) claim more lives each year than all forms of cancer and respiratory diseases combined.

Cardio exercise is beneficial because it serves to strengthen the heart by using oxygen (through your breathing) to better oxygenate the blood, which is then pumped throughout the body. Cardio also helps to regulate your heart rate and allow the beating of the heart to be fluid and less labor-intensive.

Larger-sized bodies require the heart to pump more frequently, often creating a strain on the heart due to excessive workload. If you are obese, for example, the heart has to work much harder.

Fat doesn't require oxygenated blood to take up space and so, when the heart is pumping blood to fat, it's essentially wasting time and using unnecessary beats to do the work. When you are healthy and leaner (more muscle mass than fat), your heart doesn't have to work as hard and the heartbeats are more efficient, creating less strain.

Running or walking on a treadmill allows for conditioning of the heart. This causes the walls of the heart to become stronger and the beats more efficient. Cardio improves heart health, but weight training creates muscle, which is more critical in weight loss.

Muscles require more calories and allow the body to become more efficient at burning fat. Cardio creates blood flow, but doesn't create muscle. In fact, it can strip muscle away (a more common occurrence in endurance athletes).

Exertion is what determines heart rate and also calorie burn. Trainers teach their clients to max their target heart rate to burn the most calories. In lay terms, that means you should learn your normal heart rate and move the beats per minute 70-85 percent higher than normal.

The theory is the body burns more calories and helps in weight loss and overall wellness.

But unlike other organs, the heart has a life separate from the physical, as it is deeply connected to the emotional in most societies. When we think of love, we think of the heart. The butterflies and the physical pain we experience in finding and losing love are referred to as "heartfelt".

Kathy Magliato, a cardiothoracic surgeon, talks about her journey to becoming a heart specialist in her interview with SoulPancake, a YouTube channel that features profound work in social sciences.

Dr. Magliato said she was called into the operating room by a fellow doctor who needed her help in holding the heart while he placed tiny sutures following a procedure. She said she scrubbed in with great anticipation, ready to follow the doctor's orders. Her hands were fairly large, but she found they were the perfect size to hold the human heart.

As she held the heart in her hands, she was mesmerized by the beating it continued to do while separated from the body. She was so affected by this, she decided to follow the path of becoming a cardiothoracic surgeon.

I have watched this interview several times and was captivated by the way Dr. Magliato talked about the heart. She told the story of Barney Clark, recipient of the world's first artificial heart, and the conversation physicians had with his wife.

Barney's wife had only one question when the doctors came to her husband's room to explain how the procedure would work to keep him alive.

'Will he know how to love?' She asked.

The heart is the only organ in the body that we give emotional characteristics to and think of it as having emotions. We associate it with new love as it flutters and races after we meet someone who makes us feel special; we say it hurts and feels as though it's breaking after love has left us.

Dr. Magliato goes on to explain a condition of the heart known as "Broken Heart Syndrome". According to WebMD, this is known as Takotsubo cardiomyopathy, or stress cardiomyopathy, in which there is a sudden temporary weakening of the muscular portion of the heart.

This weakening can be triggered by emotional stress (such as the death of a loved one), a break-up, rejection from a partner, or constant anxiety, leading to its more common name, Broken Heart Syndrome.

Some studies show that when one spouse dies, within a short period of time the other spouse is more likely to die due to the emotional and physical loss of their loved one. Johnny Cash died in September 2003, just five months after his wife, June Carter Cash, died. It happens more often than we think.

Harold and Ruth Knapke, of Dayton, Ohio, were married sixty-five years. Both lived in a nursing home and died eleven hours apart. Other stories of similar couples abound.

Dr. Magliato said, although, there is no scientific evidence, she believes that the soul resides in the heart. She has been bedside when patients expired and said there is a remarkable difference in their countenance when they pass. Her belief is that if the soul resides in the heart, death frees it.

The heart is suspected to have only a certain number of beats, according to Magliato, and that number, which may or may not be predetermined, is truly a mystery.

In terms of wellness, it is within such belief and mystery that I find health is critical to ensuring every beat counts. The heart is employed to give life and therefore, should be treated with great care.

The emotional component creates a dynamic about the heart that makes it unlike any other organ, and not only elevates its importance, but the consideration of the care it needs.

I have one particular client who has suffered with a heart condition since she was very young. She's had several heart surgeries and relies on medication and a fairly physically conservative lifestyle to preserve her health.

She was given permission to undertake a significant walking program and could do yoga and Pilates, which is where we would focus once she hired me to be her trainer.

As I got to know Noreen better, I realized she had suffered more than just a physical trauma to her heart. She had also suffered an emotional one. Her marriage of thirty years ended when she learned her husband was leaving her for a younger woman with whom he had been having an affair.

Noreen had been part of an affluent family from Seattle and enjoyed a lavish lifestyle. When she divorced, she moved away from Seattle, made new friends, and created a new life for herself.

But she said she would never date or marry again. She also had the kind of helping heart that wants to take care of others. She had help with her daily needs, like cleaning and grocery shopping, which gave her time to assist others in need.

I worked with Noreen for more than five years. Our sessions varied, based on how she was feeling. Sometimes it just involved sitting and talking because she was too weak from her heart issues to do anything else.

Noreen had been through a tough marriage and an even more difficult divorce. She had suffered through verbal, mental, and some physical abuse. Her divorce took more than three years to finalize, and although it has been several years, she has still never dated.

Instead, she helped me navigate through my own divorce, giving me advice on dealing with certain situations that had similar elements to her own life.

Though older now, she was still a beautiful woman with hair the color of sunshine, a flawless complexion, and deep-set blue eyes. Despite her heart condition, she was in good shape, and although she couldn't exercise like others, she maintained her healthy weight and looked great.

I never understood why she decided not to date or marry again as she could have been swept off her feet by a charming man. I once witnessed it.

Out on the town for dinner, I noticed a well-dressed older gentleman make a direct line to our table and ask Noreen if she would like to dance. She laughed it off and said she wouldn't. Yet, he didn't give up. She finally agreed to a dance and seemed to enjoy herself the rest of the night. But that was the end of it.

I didn't ask Noreen why she chose not to marry or even date again because she seemed happy and content taking care of others. I know from my own experience how heartbreak can create genuine fear and wondered if that was one of the reasons she avoided it. I'll never know.

But I suspected it had something to do with the emotional toll on her heart; a form of "Broken Heart Syndrome" from which she never recovered.

Noreen gave me great advice during my divorce and my subsequent transition to a life of my own, but I was always sad she hadn't taken a chance on finding that high school sweetheart or dancing with a stranger, not knowing the outcome.

***

Being brave plays a factor in lengthening life and allowing it to be more fulfilling. I know the times I have needed to use my brave to bust through my fear; the beats per minute of my heart were rapid.

The moment for those who are afraid of heights comes when you stand at the edge of a building and look down. As your knees grow weak and your heart beats fast, you think it might actually pop out of your chest.

Or the moment comes when you stand on the high dive and see how small the pool is below. It comes when you walk up to that stranger and wonder if they will say yes when you ask if they want to dance; when you tell the supervisor on your job that his idea isn't going to work and you have a better idea.

Your heart and your head create a delicate dance. As you begin to utilize your brave, the dance can change from awkward chaos to more of a waltz or a foxtrot as the music slows down and you settle into a peaceful, floating sensation.

My goal as a trainer is to help clients connect more with their hearts. When people decide to change their lives and their bodies, each day is like a step off the high dive until real progress shows up.

Stepping on the scale can be like standing on the edge of the Grand Canyon with no barrier to protect you. Fear is the motivator to change and to not stay the same. The heart teaches us during those moments when your heart beats fast.

The heart, when treated as both a vital organ for life and the home of the soul, can create opportunity and vitality for a life to be lived more fully and being brave requires that you take chances.

I remember when I was training for the Ironman, my body ached everywhere, but my heart was full, as I was doing something I had dreamed about for years.

I have listened as people told stories of having put off the things that they wanted to do in their lives but didn't because they didn't have time or couldn't make space for it. Instead, they settled for average.

When that happens to you, remember that the heart is a muscle and requires pressure (like other muscles) to build and get stronger. You will get stronger after a good session at the gym, or after an anxious meeting when you said your peace and were listened to.

It is often overlooked as a muscle because there is no specific exercise machine for the heart, but everything you do affects the heart. One way to know if it's working well is to do things outside the norm. Being brave (and unafraid), showing love and compassion, and reaching out and connecting with others can help work our hearts, too.

Maintaining good fitness habits and taking care of our bodies can actually help us get to know our hearts better and allow us to take risks in life we might not take otherwise.

Nick, from chapter one, was a young man who hid his heart behind his fat. He knew if people didn't like him because he was fat, then that was okay. But if he wasn't fat and they didn't like him, that would be much harder to accept.

He used his weight to build a wall around his heart—a wall that could have eventually killed him. When he began to lose weight and saw that people liked him because he let them get to know him better, his heart began to get stronger.

His health also began to improve and the wall built to protect his heart began to disappear.

Physically, the walls of fat would have snuffed out the heart. Emotionally, the walls would isolate it. Nick exposing his heart, allowed it the freedom to beat faster and find a new rhythm.

Alice Montgomery, my sweet Southern friend, led with her heart but always gave more to others than to herself. She was so wrapped up in caring for others, it was like being on a treadmill going nowhere for hours. Her heartbeats were for others and not for herself.

When she needed to use the heart to fuel herself, she found her heart couldn't turn its attention on her alone. That was too "selfish".

***

Interval training is the best form of exercise that allows both the heart and body to receive an extremely beneficial workout. Interval training is a combination of cardio and weight training and is said to be the best type of training today. CrossFit, Orange Theory, F45, Tabata, and a number of other small boutique-like wellness centers have been built on this concept.

The idea is that short bursts of high-intensity cardio followed by short bursts of weight training is the most effective technique for overall well-being. That's why there is a noticeable difference in triathletes and endurance runners, also in sprinters and marathon runners. Sprinters are significantly more muscular and marathon runners are very lean. However, they all subscribe to interval training.

One simple example is two minutes of jump rope, followed by one minute of weighted squats, followed by one minute of rest. This allows the heart to beat faster by using the oxygenated blood and oxygen itself to build muscle and burn fat over shorter periods of time.

This simple routine allows the body to pull from fat as a fuel source due to the demand from the shorter bursts of high intensity, as well as being more effective for losing fat and gaining muscle. When we push ourselves, find our brave, and use fear as a challenge, we can begin to build that muscle—the one that tells you to take that first step into the unknown.

I can't count the times I told myself when I was afraid that I could do anything. I was an Ironman, after all, and when you have done an Ironman, you can theoretically do anything. I have a crazy fear of heights and despite jumping out of an airplane twice, I still can't stand heights.

In Boone, North Carolina, there is a place called Grandfather Mountain with a suspension bridge built in 1952. This mile-high bridge is famous because it's the highest in America and links two peaks together. It's called the swinging bridge because in the wind it sways.

Some visitors, afraid of heights like me, would crawl across on their hands and knees. It has been updated and swings much less, but is still a scary experience for me.

In 2003, shortly after moving to Asheville, our family took a trip to Grandfather Mountain. I could not find the courage to cross that bridge and even winced and trembled at the idea of my husband taking my kids across it.

In 2019, I returned with my two children with one task—to cross that swinging bridge. I wanted to prove to myself that I could do it—and conquer my fear. I felt that bridge had made its mark on me.

As I approached the bridge, I could feel all of my muscles tensing up, my knees beginning to knock, and my heart pounding out of my chest. I knew the reality was that no one had fallen off the bridge and no one had died while on the bridge, but my body shook as though it were the very end of my life.

I knew that crossing had more to do with using the power of my own perception and the power of having done greater feats.

I crossed the bridge with great effort, strengthening my heart in the process.

I needed to be able to show my own mind and spirit that the limitations I believed in were in fact a poison. I know crossing a bridge or completing an Ironman won't make me more successful in life, but they will allow me to believe I can do anything I set my mind to do, as I have before.

The heart, when challenged, like any other muscle, causes it to get stronger. Yet, we seem unable to give the same effort to emotional heart work as we do to physical heart work.

It is my belief the heart can grow stronger, not just from being on a treadmill for an hour of cardio, but from doing things that inspire fear and things that excite you—like asking that special someone out, committing to jumping out of an airplane, or tackling a certain task you may be afraid of.

Simply put, the heart needs more than just cardio to get stronger and find the boundaries of brave. Facing and overcoming your fears is another way to do just that.

Strangely enough, when training clients, I saw time and again people protecting themselves, unwilling to really dig deep, possibly fall in love, or take chances. Pain good or bad allows us to live a little more and become better people.

When you are in pain, you know you are alive. Sweet pain is what we call the pain when you are sore after a good lift. It is a "good" pain that makes you aware that you are really doing the work.

Cardio causes the heart stress, but a good stress. It causes the type of irregular beat that over time becomes regular. When you create the kind of stress in your body from doing sprints, taking the stairs, walking uphill, or jogging on a treadmill, you allow your body to learn to adapt.

Over time, it will carve out the capacity for deeper, more meaningful breaths.

I have solved a number of problems on a cardio machine, been creative, conjured the possibilities of new businesses, and had countless conversations with people in my head while covering miles on a conveyor belt to nowhere. I can say my heart is stronger and beats better because of it.

Ironically, the way to strengthen the heart is to expose it to stress and physical activity.

Life and love are risky, both holding the same truths that they don't last forever.

Before each session with my clients, I have them get on a treadmill or bike and do five to seven minutes of a warm-up. I am sometimes asked if this is to prevent injury, and although it is, the goal is to allow my clients time to focus and leave the day outside the gym.

I hope during the time they are on the treadmill, I can get them to invest more in themselves as a means to reach better heart health, live better, and live longer.

Being brave isn't the absence of fear. It's doing something even if it scares you. What small steps can you take now to move the boundaries of brave into a whole new, bigger, better, and stronger you?

Epilogue

Books are written for many different reasons and in many different ways. In my case, I didn't publish this book because I had a compelling story of overcoming great obstacles in life.

I didn't sleep in my car after being homeless. I didn't lose everything, or suffer from an eating disorder to become a health expert. I didn't lose a hundred pounds and change my life completely.

What I did instead was almost let the best years of my life slip past because of complacency. I have since learned, after living almost half my life, that what can rob you of the best years of your life is the deadness of complacency.

Mediocrity is what happens when the risk of failing is too great. "I am doing my best at eating and exercising, but I'm not perfect. Sometimes I cheat", or "It's not my dream job, but it pays the bills".

These are the same sentences I have used throughout my own life. Complacency sneaks up and stays a while. It lurks like a shadow, reminding us that being mediocre is okay and being brave is scary.

Over the years, these beliefs can become our lifelong companions, preventing us from moving forward or doing our best. Like me, you may have started and stopped a weight-loss program so many times you've lost count.

Yet, you still keep trying. That is not complacency, my friend. That is a champion!

A favorite line I've developed out of my work is: 'Helping you to make the inside and the outside match.' I know that inside each of us is a mission to make the world a better place, and that our journey here is to discover and release it.

In her book, *What's in the Way is the Way,* poet Mary O'Malley writes:

Life is set up to bring up
what is bound up so it can open up to be freed up
so you can show up for life.

I believe we all have something to contribute to this world and that our task is to determine just what that job may be. Life is coming for you, like it or not. Sometimes it's as easy as meeting an old friend, and sometimes it's as scary as the mean old man who lives down the block you have to confront every day.

Either way, life is a participatory sport. Do you have the skills to join and excel?

My fitness life has granted me permission to participate and learn more. It is in the gym I expose my limits and my capabilities, my strengths and weaknesses, my fears and my confidence to overcome them.

I hope these stories remind you there are places we can all test our brave and discover what poisonous perceptions we need to work on in our daily lives that tend to hold us back.

After almost twenty-five years in the fitness industry, I realize I had the coolest gig out there. I knew when someone was stuck, or felt stuck; I knew finding something to move them out of that place of comfort was one of the most vulnerable things they could do.

Whenever I weighed someone as a preliminary assessment to chart progress, I can't count the number of times people begin to tear up, or get uncomfortable, and want to hide under a table.

I wanted to hug everyone and tell them it was going to be okay. I believed in them and if they believed in me, we could get them to where they wanted to be.

I felt it was also my contribution and my calling to cheer for people and be their source of courage when they didn't have any of their own.

What a gift those years were for me, and how grateful I am for the many lives I was able to participate in.

Today, I am in real estate, and although it's not the same, I feel as though I help people in this business, too. I miss my clients, and I miss making a difference in the lives of those I worked with, though I still see and talk to many of them.

Nick, whom you met in chapter one, is twenty-seven now and has lost more than two hundred pounds. He gained back some of the weight he lost when we worked together, but has been able to maintain a healthier lifestyle. He looks fantastic and feels like the whole world is now open for him. He plans to move to NYC and become a fashion designer.

I can only hope that my touching his life meant a door opened for him. That he walked through it was entirely due to him.

One of the things I have learned through watching people change their physical lives is that as their body gets smaller, their dreams get bigger. You can achieve more than you ever knew when you achieve something you never thought you could.

As you reflect on *How Big is Your Brave?*, I pray that you find comfort, solace, and inspiration in the stories shared within these pages.

It's when you are willing to step out and step up into the world, open your arms wide, and yell, "How big is my brave?" that you are truly displaying your courage.

And courage, as a wise man once said, is being the *only* one who knows you are afraid.